D0773720

Changing Children's Behavior Quickly

NATIONAL UNIVERSITY
LIBRARY   SAN DIEGO

Changing Children's Behavior Quickly

Richard L. Munger

MADISON BOOKS

Copyright © 1993 by Richard L. Munger

All rights reserved.
No part of this book may be reproduced in any form or
by any electronic or mechanical means, including
information storage and retrieval systems, without
written permission from the publisher, except by a
reviewer who may quote passages in a review.

Published by Madison Books
4720 Boston Way
Lanham, Maryland 20706

Distributed by National Book Network

The paper used in this publication meets the minimum
requirements of American National Standard for
Information Sciences—Permanence of Paper for
Printed Library Materials, ANSI Z39.48–1984. ∞™
Manufactured in the United States of America.

Library of Congress Cataloging-in-Publication Data

Munger, Richard L.
Changing children's behavior quickly / Richard L.
Munger.
p. cm.
Includes index.
1. Problem children—Behavior modification.
2. Discipline of children. I. Title.
RJ506.P63M86   1993
649'.64—dc20   92–45814 CIP

ISBN 1–56833–001–4 (alk. paper)

To my grandparents

Contents

Acknowledgments

Special thanks to Paul Rossman for the splendid illustrations in this book and to Elaine Marcus and Tom Bensman for their assistance with design and editing. My thanks also to Trent Hicks for the use of the *Daily Report Card* in Chapter 4 and to the Adam Walsh Child Resource Center of Fort Lauderdale, Florida, for the *Child Safety Tips* in Chapter 7. Finally, I am grateful to Sheila Cromer, R.N., for reviewing the book's medical discussions for accuracy.

Preface

✍ *A Note to Professionals*

Many parenting books and curricula require either time-consuming workshops or a great deal of effort and/or literacy of the consumers. There is a need to present behavior management techniques in a format that is both accessible and comprehensible to families unable to benefit from traditional resources. This book is a response to that need.

Changing Children's Behavior Quickly takes some of the most successful techniques in child management, boils them down to a bare minimum, and packages them in a way to engage frustrated parents. Written on an easy reading level, this book contains many charts, checklists, and illustrations to help parents master the approaches.

Although parents are the ultimate consumers of this book, the initial audience for its use is the thousands of social service, mental health, juvenile justice, and education professionals around the country who provide parents with training in child management. This book will be especially relevant to professionals who work in family preservation and home-based services programs. It gives professionals a new and timely resource to engage parents whom they seek to help daily in their agencies.

Introduction for Parents

Some parents may feel that the approaches and methods I recommend in this book are too controlling and uncaring. These parents would prefer a more "humanistic" approach to raising children. I think such a belief is fine, so let me explain why I think the program outlined in this book fits into a humanistic approach to raising children.

Both younger children and adolescents need clear behavioral limits regarding what they can and cannot do. If you think children are happy with lots of freedom and control over you, then you are wrong. Professionals who study children all agree on this issue: children feel safe and loved within firm, fair behavioral boundaries. Testing those boundaries is the normal, healthy way children discover and learn about appropriate and inappropriate behavior. Therefore, testing limits is natural and good. If parents do not set clear limits, or if they enforce limits inconsistently, then something very important happens: children get anxious. It may or may not show on the surface, but the child, inside, becomes anxious, or unsettled, about having too much power and control in setting his or her own limits. Then what happens with all that anxiety? It usually stirs up the child into further acting out against and testing of limits. It causes the child to push more and more against what few limits there might be. This increasing "misbehavior" is how children deal with the anxiety of inconsistent, unclear, or too few limits on their behavior. You, as parents, must establish limits, and in doing so, you will create a safe, supportive environment for your children. It is only then, in my experience, that all the other things involved in bringing up children will work. This book will guide you in setting basic limits, which is the first step toward humanistic child rearing.

This book is meant to help you change your child's (or children's) problem behaviors as quickly as possible, using simple techniques that will work with most children. Unfortunately, most approaches taught in workshops and books for parents are time-consuming and/or expensive, and they often require much effort to learn. Although many of these approaches are excellent, I feel there is a great need for an alternative program that:

❑ Can be learned quickly—in this case, by reading a few chapters and completing some lists.

❑ Can be used immediately after it is learned; requires little practice.

❑ Gives quick results. When parents consult with a professional or a publication, they typically are emotionally at their "wits' end"; they need to see success quickly for, if nothing else, their own mental condition. Also, in many cases, the child's behavior is getting out of control and may be quite dangerous.

❑ Works with most problem behaviors, even difficult ones that parents have not been able to change through spanking, grounding, taking away privileges, or other methods.

This book is made up of nine chapters; you can read any or all chapters, depending on the needs of your child. Chapters 1 and 2 help you set up a discipline program for children and teenagers of all ages. Chapter 3 discusses a specific discipline technique you can use with young children, aged 2–12, instead of some of the usual punishments parents have tried with their children. Chapter 4 is about school problems and how you can motivate your child toward better academic and behavioral adjustment in educational settings. Chapters 5 through 9 deal with specific childhood issues: communication, hyperactivity, life-styles, divorce, and bedwetting.

Recently, a 14-year-old girl who was acting out, creating havoc in her family, rebelling against every possible limit, and cursing the world for its unfairness said to me on the edge of tears: "Mom doesn't even care enough to make me do it." In over fifteen years of work with youths and their families, I have never met a parent who didn't really care. Parents care, I know, and this book is meant to help parents show that they care and avoid situations like that of the 14-year-old girl.

Can This Book Help You?

The discipline and behavior change plans discussed in this book have been shown to be useful when learned in clinical settings, that is, with a professional counselor. In general, studies of self-help approaches such as this one have shown that about 50% of people using programs on their own are helped. If you are not successful in following this program on your own, you should consider talking to a professional in your community, for example, your child's school guidance counselor.

A Special Note About Sex

I'll discuss the issue of sexuality in Chapter 7; here, I mean the use of masculine and feminine pronouns. I have been greatly confused by the "he-she" problem. I am totally in sympathy with the view that women often feel put down by the use of "he" in reference to a person in general. However, I find a "himself-herself" in the middle of a sentence to be disruptive. Until someone comes up with a set of nonsexual pronouns, there is no good solution to the problem. Therefore, I have chosen to deal with the problem by making all general references in female terms in one chapter, and in masculine terms in the next. Chapters 1 and 2 are related and so use female pronouns when the reference is general; the third chapter uses masculine pronouns for the same purpose, and so on throughout the book.

Chapter 1
Rules for Unruly Children

I find that in about 80% of the cases in which I consult with parents about discipline problems at home, the child has actually become the boss around the house; the child is controlling the parents. One purpose of this chapter is to put the power back where it belongs, in the hands of the parents, who are attempting to raise their children with all good intentions.

Many years of research on child development have shown that children need behavior limits. This program will help you set such limits for your child. As soon as you set those limits, they can be easily enforced through the use of this program. Quite simply, this program can enable you to be the boss in your own home again.

Learning Good Behavior

This program is based on the idea that children *learn* to behave correctly. The word "learn" is emphasized because it is important. You may be upset because you think your child should know how to behave correctly. Although this is understandable—it is a common assumption—it is wrong: children do not instinctively know how to behave. At least for now, please follow me with a different assumption: *children learn to behave correctly, specifically by seeing that good behavior is rewarded.*

Your child simply needs a more structured approach to help her *learn* that good behavior will earn rewards. This program structures your child's life so that she knows what to expect as a consequence of her actions. It makes life more predictable for her. Only within this structure will discipline be consistent so that your child can *learn* to behave correctly. It is essential that you help her to *learn* good behavior. To do that, you need to give her rewards for good behavior.

This program is for children and adolescents from about age 5 to age 18. It is a collection of techniques that are not new; I am simply putting them into a package that will help you, as parents, learn to use them more easily. You may already do many of the things in this book, but perhaps your methods need to be fine-tuned—perhaps you need to be more consistent with them. Perhaps you need to focus on making rules ahead of time instead of after the fact. These two points about the fine-tuning of disciplinary techniques will be discussed later.

Parents must be in control; not the child!

Zeroing in on Problem Behaviors

On this page, list all of your child's problem behaviors. Include those behaviors that she does too often, for example, fighting, and also include those behaviors that she needs to do more often, for example, cleaning her room. There is space for at least eight behaviors, so please take your time and list as many problem behaviors as you can.

Make a list of all your child's problem behaviors.

Problem Behaviors

Example: *She comes home too late.*

1.

2.

3.

4.

5.

6.

7.

8.

On this page, make a list of the three or four problem behaviors that you think are most necessary to change in your child, that is, the ones that are most important to you. Go back to your first list of problem behaviors and review it carefully. Choose only those three or four problem behaviors that you want to change the most. Include them on the target behaviors list. Think carefully; which behaviors are most important to you?

Target Behaviors

Make a list of the three or four problem behaviors (from the previous page) that you most want to change now, that is, the ones that are most important to you.

Target Behaviors

Example: *She talks back to me.*

1.

2.

3.

4.

Your Child's Needs

In order to get the behavior they want from their children, parents must identify and control certain things the children value. Parents must be "in charge of the chips," so to speak. However, it is important to know the difference between what a child really needs and what a child merely wants or desires. Desires can be used as bargaining chips—needs should never be.

On this page, you will see a list of what are called "basic privileges." These are needs that a child should get "free"—no strings attached. The first is food. This is obvious, but as noted on the list, only essential, nutritious food counts as a basic privilege. It does not include snacks, special desserts, or any favorite foods that you always keep in the refrigerator for the child, such as ice cream or Cokes. Another obvious free privilege (or basic privilege, as I am calling them) is shelter. A third is clothing, and, again, it is noted on the list that only essential clothing is included. Expensive and popular designer jeans, special Nike running shoes, and similar kinds of things are not included. Finally, there is love, a basic privilege I do not need to say any more about.

Basic Privileges

⇨ **Food** (only nutritious food; does not include snacks, special desserts, favorite foods around the house, such as ice cream, etc.)

⇨ **Shelter** (a safe home environment, with some private space.)

⇨ **Clothing** (only essential clothing; does not include designer jeans, Nikes, etc.)

⇨ **Love**

Children should always receive the four basic privileges free. There is one more addition to the "free" list—a "growth privilege." Growth privileges are activities that are important, even essential, to a child's growth. They should not, therefore, be treated as optional privileges; they should never be withdrawn regardless of the child's behavior. Some examples of growth privileges are Boy Scouts and Girl Scouts, music and ballet lessons, church youth groups, 4-H Clubs, and extracurricular activities at school, including, of course, athletics. A child may sometimes need special encouragement to participate in growth activities. In such cases, you may want to encourage participation by making a rule that earns a certain privilege for participating in the activity.

Below is space to make another list. List some growth privileges for your child. Again, these are activities that you think are necessary for your child's growth. There is room for four; try to list at least several important growth activities for your child.

Growth Privileges
Make a list of activities that you think are essential to your child's growth. These growth privileges should always be available and should never be taken away for bad behavior.

Growth Privileges

Example: *Girl Scouts*

1.

2.

3.

4.

**"Growth privileges" are
always available to the child, free.**

Optional Privileges, or Rewards

All privileges that are not "basic" are considered "optional." As such, they should never be given free—they should be earned. Giving optional privileges for free is one of the most common mistakes parents make, and this program is designed to help correct this problem.

Because they should be earned, optional privileges are also often called "rewards." This type of privilege includes things, activities, praise, and tokens. An example of a thing is a specific food reward, such as a candy bar. An example of an activity privilege is going to a movie. Praise or attention is valued by people of all ages, especially younger children and teenagers. An example of a token is a certificate of some type that the child can exchange for a desired reward. Tokens come in handy when you wish to use a large reward that you can't give every day, such as a lunch trip to McDonald's.

In this program, you must choose privileges that are highly desirable to your child. Each child is different, and as your child's parent, you have the best idea of what she wants. Another thing to remember: the younger the child, the more frequently she has to be rewarded. It is important that the child see the positive benefits of good behavior by frequent rewards.

Optional Privileges: Basic Principles

⇨ Optional privileges must be earned.

⇨ Optional privileges (also called "rewards") may be things, activities, tokens, or praise.

⇨ Choose rewards that are highly desired by your child.

⇨ The younger the child, the more frequently she has to be rewarded.

⇨ It is important for the child to see the positive results of her good behavior by frequent rewards.

On the next page is a short list of some sample optional privileges, or rewards. Rewards will differ from child to child and also for the same child at different ages. In addition to the more standard rewards in the list, larger rewards, such as horseback riding lessons, an old (but safe) clunker car that Father would be willing to purchase, or perhaps a weekend trip, are sometimes appropriate for special behavior or a longer period of desired behavior. Young children often view special activities with a parent (or parents) as rewarding; such activities include fishing, going to a park or playground, swimming, and attending a football game. Teenagers, on the other hand, generally put more value on time spent with their peers.

Optional privileges should be earned.

Sample Optional Privileges

For young children:
After-school snack
Dessert
Going outside after dinner
Going to McDonald's
Having a favorite meal
Having a friend stay overnight
Playing with the Nintendo
Special activity with a parent
Use of bike
Watching TV

For teenagers:
Dating
Going shopping
Going to the movies
Listening to the stereo
Nonbasic clothes
Staying up past normal bedtime
Telephone time
Use of car
Watching TV
Watching videos

Regarding the use of tokens as rewards, below you will see a list of three different kinds of token systems. Tokens may be objects, such as poker chips. One advantage of this is that you can use a point system with the colors, if you desire. You can also make up your own point system for tokens. In this case, you would need to record these points on a chart that you make up. Finally, you can use certificates. Below is a sample certificate with a space at the bottom where you can write in what thing the child can earn by cashing in the certificate.

Sample Tokens

☐ Poker chips. Different colors can have different values, e.g., blue = 1; red = 5; white = 10.

☐ Points. Use a chart to record these. A sample chart appears on page 136.

☐ Certificates. See example below.

**Children may cash in earned
certificates for desired privileges.**

Your Child's Desires

Below, make a list of optional privileges—things your child likes but doesn't absolutely need. In many cases, your child may already be getting these free, but you should include them here anyway. Think back to the basic privileges; if something is not food, shelter, clothing, love, or a growth activity, it should appear on this list; almost anything your child likes can be considered an optional privilege. Again, there is space for a number of responses, and you should think this through carefully, listing as many things as you can that your child finds rewarding.

Make a list of optional privileges, that is, things and activities your child likes. Although your child may already be getting some of them "free," include all privileges your child likes that are not basic privileges.

Optional Privileges

1.

2.

3.

4.

5.

6.

7.

Now choose three or four of the optional privileges (from the list you just made) that are most desired by your child. Try to think of the things or activities that motivate your child the most. Put them in order, with the most desired first.

Most Desired Privileges
Choose three or four of the privileges from your previous list of optional privileges that are *most* desired by your child. Rank them in order, with the most desired first.

1.

2.

3.

4.

Rule Making
Rules are the exact opposite of a child's problem behaviors. A rule takes a problem behavior and states it as the positive behavior a parent desires. There are several points to discuss about rules. First, never make too many rules. Only a very few rules can be regularly enforced. In this program, we are going to start with three or four rules that cover only the most important problem behaviors of your child.

A rule must be very clear. All possible loopholes must be plugged up by making rules very specific, because children will always test for loopholes. For example, some parents had a rule allowing their teenager to earn a movie on Friday or Saturday night if she did her list of chores each week. Unfortunately, there was only one movie theater in town, and one weekend it was showing an "R"-rated movie. Using much wisdom, the parents decided to explain that they had made a mistake and had not written the rule to be specific enough. Clearly, a movie could be earned only if it were rated "G," "PG," or "PG-13." The rule was rewritten to include that change, and the teenager was given a special onetime $5 reward to make up for missing the movie.

A rule should be so clear and specific that anyone (a baby-sitter, for example) should be able to tell whether the rule has been followed. Below is an example of a very specific rule. As you can see, the rule is written like a law. In writing a new law, the lawmakers must always define what each word means. You must do the same for a rule.

Example Rule

☞ Rule: *You must be in the house at 6:00 P.M. on weekdays.*

❑ "You" means all the children who live here (not Mom and not Dad).

❑ "Must be" means that you will lose your privilege to operate electronic things, such as TV, radio, and telephone, for the rest of that evening and the entire next day if you are late.

❑ "In the house" means both feet inside any of the following doors: front door, side door, basement door.

❑ "At 6:00 P.M." means six in the afternoon, on the same day, as indicated by the telephone time lady.

❑ "On weekdays" means Sunday through Thursday.

❑ The total rule is in effect whenever your mother, father, or the sitter is in the house at 6:00 P.M. or from the time after 6:00 P.M. that he or she arrives home.

This rule may seem silly to some people. However, a rule does not have to seem important to anyone but the rulemaker, who is, of course, very interested in enforcement of that rule. To be effective, a rule must be enforced every time it is broken. Rules will always be tested by children, so parents must be prepared to enforce the rules they make.

In writing a rule, it is often useful to get the child's ideas. Important information may be discovered that will help you write a better rule. If you get the child's ideas, you will find that in many cases she is willing to do far more than you would ask in return for something she wants very much. Sometimes you may be willing, too, to give your child a special privilege in return for extra-good behavior. However, once a rule is written, it is not open for discussion, unless the rulemaker wants to change it.

A rule does not have to pass a fairness test, either, but it must be possible for the child to carry out. Finally, parents must realize that not all rules are for all members of the family. It is not necessary to enforce a "problem" rule for those who are mature enough to practice self-control. Therefore, be very specific about who must follow the rule.

This chapter is most concerned about rules to correct problem behaviors, but rules can also encourage positive behaviors (sometimes called "prosocial behaviors"). An example is a parent who wants her child to attend the church youth group. If the child resists, the parent can make a rule that if the child goes to the weekly group, she can get some very desired privilege. Of course, the child still has the choice of not attending and not getting the privilege. It is important, though, to provide the child with chances to earn important privileges in return for very good behaviors, above and beyond normal everyday expectations.

Now we are ready to start making rules. Look back at page 4, where you listed three or four major problem behaviors of your child that you want to target. Think of a rule about the first targeted problem behavior. Try to express the rule *positively*. Here is an example of how to write a rule in a positive way: Let's say the number one problem on the list is fighting with a sister. Instead of making the rule "no fighting with your sister," make the rule into a positive one such as "playing with your sister will be respectful and will involve no hurtful touching." You may also have to add a description of inappropriate behavior, but again, try to emphasize the positive.

For Rule #1 on the next page, write a rule concerning your child's number one problem behavior. Just take your time and do your best. When you are writing the rule, be sure to write all the parts to it. Look back to page 13 again for an example of how to be very clear about defining what a rule means. Be just as clear with your rule. Make your list underneath the rule, and take plenty of time.

Next, look at your rule and run it through the rule checklist on the same page. If you can answer "yes" to a checklist question, then check it off. If not, go back and rewrite the rule—add to it or clarify it—so that it will pass the checklist. Can you enforce the rule 100% of the time? Have you clearly defined the expected behavior, that is, said exactly what you want the child to do? "Clean the house once a week" is not specific enough about the expected behavior. What does "clean the house" mean? Is the rule very specific?

Finally, check the rule for any possible loopholes. A common loophole concerns where the child must be at curfew time. Children will often find a loophole, so they will be home in time, but they will not be in the house. They might be out in front of the house talking with a friend. That is an example of a loophole that you would need to close up by defining more clearly what the curfew means. For example, "be inside the house, inside the doors to the house, by 10:00 P.M."

When you have completed the checklist, rewrite the rule at the bottom of the page. There is plenty of space to do it. Write a very clear, good rule. Most rules are, in fact, several sentences long. Take as much time and space as you need.

Rule #1

Unpolished Rule:

Be very specific and list all parts to the rule. Define each word, or part, clearly.

1.

2.

3.

4.

5.

6.

7.

8.

Rule checklist:

✔ Is it enforceable 100% of the time?
✔ Is the expected behavior clearly defined?
✔ Is the rule very specific?
✔ Have all loopholes been plugged?

Final Rule:

When you have finished the first rule, go on to the next pages and complete Rules #2, #3, and #4, just as you did the first rule. Write the rules to apply to target behaviors #2–#4 on page 4. Carry each rule through from the writing of the unpolished rule and its very specific parts, to the checklist, and, finally, to the writing of the final rule at the bottom of the page. This should take you at least fifteen minutes. It should be done very carefully, because these rules will be the basis of further discussion, so take your time.

Rule #2

Unpolished Rule:

Be very specific and list all parts to the rule. Define each word, or part, clearly.

1.

2.

3.

4.

5.

6.

7.

8.

Rule checklist:

✔ Is it enforceable 100% of the time?
✔ Is the expected behavior clearly defined?
✔ Is the rule very specific?
✔ Have all loopholes been plugged?

Final Rule:

Rule #3

Unpolished Rule:

Be very specific and list all parts to the rule. Define each word, or part, clearly.

1.

2.

3.

4.

5.

6.

7.

8.

Rule checklist:

✔ Is it enforceable 100% of the time?
✔ Is the expected behavior clearly defined?
✔ Is the rule very specific?
✔ Have all loopholes been plugged?

Final Rule:

Rule #4

Unpolished Rule:

Be very specific and list all parts to the rule. Define each word, or part, clearly.

1.

2.

3.

4.

5.

6.

7.

8.

Rule checklist:

✔ Is it enforceable 100% of the time?
✔ Is the expected behavior clearly defined?
✔ Is the rule very specific?
✔ Have all loopholes been plugged?

Final Rule:

Your Child's Behavior Agreement

It is now time to introduce the Family Contract. Below is a Family Contract form. On the left-hand side of the page, in the Rule column, write the rules that you have just completed: #1–#4. After you have finished, at the bottom of the page, where it says "Growth privileges," write in the growth privileges that you have decided on for your child. (See page 6 for a reminder.) You are now halfway to a contract.

Family Contract

Post on Refrigerator

Rule	Privilege
1.	1.
2.	2.
3.	3.
4.	4.

Growth privileges:

Date: _____

Signatures: _____

_____

_____

Look back at page 12, where you listed your child's most desired privileges. You are going to link these privileges to your four rules. For example, with the first rule, the child will be getting a particular privilege if she follows the rule. Write this privilege down in the Family Contract. Be very careful that it is written positively so that the child has the privilege as long as she follows the rule. If the child doesn't follow the rule, the privilege is not given for a day or two, or even a week. The amount of "penalty" time for breaking each rule needs to be stated very clearly in the Family Contract. The next couple of pages contain some sample Family Contracts that may help you as you work on your contract.

Just a note about writing rules and privileges in a positive form: You have already tried to write your rules in a positive way and you should also always try to put your privileges in the same positive form. An example of this is privilege #1 in Sample Family Contract #1 on the next page. Obviously, according to the way this rule is written, if the child is late and comes home after the curfew, she is going to be restricted as a result. However, look at how the privilege is worded: "Activities outside the house." On a school night, the child is free to go outside and do what she pleases. This is a privilege that the child is allowed as long as she follows the rules. If she does not follow the rule, then she will not be allowed the privilege of leaving the house for the next two school nights.

Sample Family Contract #1   *Post on Refrigerator*

Rule	Privilege
1. Curfew is 10 P.M. on school nights (Sunday through Thursday). This means you must be in the house.	1. Activities outside the house. For each 30 minutes past curfew, you will be restricted to the house for the next two school nights.
2. Curfew is 12 P.M. on non–school nights. This means you must be in the house.	2. Activities outside the house. For each 15 minutes past curfew, you will be restricted to the house for the next non–school night.
3. Take out trash every Monday night before going to bed.	3. Use of TV on Tuesday night.
4. Study school assignments for one hour after dinner, Sunday night through Thursday night, at the desk in your room. No radio or other distraction.	4. Use of TV or radio that night.

Growth privileges: church youth group, baseball team

Date: _____

Signatures: _____   _____

Sample Family Contract #2   *Post on Refrigerator*

Rule	Privilege
1. Respectful talk and behavior toward stepmother and father. Examples of nonrespect: talking back, throwing things, raising voice when corrected.	1. Go to game room or movie on Friday or Saturday night. (If the rule is broken during the week, privilege is lost for the coming week.)
2. Be in the house, not outside, by 6:30 P.M. on school nights (Sunday through Thursday).	2. Use the phone until 8:00 P.M. without hassling parents about when you want to use it. (If the rule is broken, privilege is lost for the remainder of that day and the next day.)
3. Study or do homework for 45 minutes on school nights.	3. See boyfriend the next school day from after school until curfew. (If the rule is broken, privilege is lost for that day and the next day. This also includes girlfriends.)
4. Chores: A. Fold clothes on wash day (not the next day); B. Polish playroom furniture by 12:00 noon on Saturday; C. Vacuum carpet in front hall and playroom by 6:00 P.M. on Wednesday and by 12:00 noon on Saturday; D. Pick up all dishes and glasses that you use, and put them in the sink.	4. Allowance of $5 on Friday at 6:30 P.M. (If the rule is broken during the week, no allowance on Friday for that week.)

Growth privileges: church youth group, baseball team

Date: _____

Signatures: _____   _____

In the contract, you should tie at least one of your child's optional privileges to each rule. In some cases, you will link to a specific rule more than one privilege that the child enjoys. A commonly used example is the privilege of "electronic things." This includes radio, television, VCR, telephone, and video games, all lumped together and tied to a specific rule.

At the bottom of the Family Contract are blanks for the date of the contract and signatures. Anyone who will be enforcing the Family Contract in the home should sign it, and so should anyone who must follow the rules. In some rare cases, your child will refuse to sign because she feels the rules are not fair. In these cases, after you have made every effort to talk with the child, just note at the bottom of the contract that she refused to sign. However, the child still must obey the rules, even if the Family Contract is not signed. (Remember: rules don't have to be fair from the child's point of view.)

Now take some time to work on your Family Contract. There are several blank practice forms on the following pages. Again, look at the samples for help.

Family Contract

Post on Refrigerator

Rule	Privilege
1.	1.
2.	2.
3.	3.
4.	4.

Growth privileges:

Date: _____

Signatures: _____

_____

_____

Family Contract

Post on Refrigerator

Rule	Privilege
1.	**1.**
2.	**2.**
3.	**3.**
4.	**4.**

Growth privileges:

Date: _____

Signatures: _____

_____

_____

Family Contract   *Post on Refrigerator*

Rule   ### Privilege

1.   **1.**

2.   **2.**

3.   **3.**

4.   **4.**

Growth privileges:

Date: _____

Signatures: _____

_____

_____

Your Role in Changing Your Child's Behavior

The enforcement of rules is a critical factor in the success of this program. First, you must enforce a rule 100% of the time. This is very important and there can be no exceptions, unless the rule has been lifted ahead of time for a special occasion. An example would be if a child needs to come in past the curfew because of involvement in a onetime church camping trip. Any regular exceptions should be written into the rule. For rare instances, however, you may decide ahead of time to lift the rule, but clearly, it must be well in advance of the special activity.

Another important point: if a rule is no longer needed and the appropriate behavior can be done without it, simply stop the rule and praise the child for her accomplishment.

Always enforce rules unemotionally and ignore any arguing or attempts at explanations. If you wrote a rule correctly, you should know if it was broken.

Expect rules to be tested. In fact, many children's behavior worsens after starting this particular program. This is a good sign; the child simply wants you to give it up. The child doesn't like it, and she will make it tough for you to enforce the contract.

Parents must agree on rules and enforce them equally. This goes for anyone who may be in charge: others living in the household, a relative living next door, or, say, a grandparent whom the child visits regularly.

After a rule is broken, always go to the contract on the refrigerator with a serious look on your face, and read the results aloud with the child. This is essential. If you don't do this, the program won't work, so do it. Even if you don't think it is important, believe me, it is—do it every time a rule is broken. Sometimes the child will be angry and will refuse to go with you. You should go anyway, telling the child that you went and what was on the Family Contract. This helps to make the program a learning experience.

Finally, if a child refuses to have a privilege withdrawn, then enforce the contract by physical withdrawal of the privilege. For example, if a child continues to watch TV, lock the TV; there are locks to do that. Sears sells a tiny lock that goes into the hole in your TV plug; it costs less than two dollars. If she won't stop riding her bike, lock up the bike. If your child breaks a rule for which you can't physically withdraw the privilege, then you may want to "up the ante." This means adding more privileges to be earned for that particular rule-behavior. Breaking the rule would mean even fewer privileges. If a child is getting only the basic privileges and perhaps a few growth privileges, after a while life will be very boring. If you stick with it, you will outlast the child.

After some experience, it will be easy for you to write a rule and select a privilege that encourages your child to behave more appropriately. However, after starting a rule, you may need to make some changes or to fine-tune the rule. For example, if you weren't clear enough with your rule, the child may find a loophole. So then you rewrite it. You also may have chosen a privilege that is not desired enough. For example, your rule may require the child to make her bed every day in order to have the privilege of watching TV after school. If the child simply listens to the radio and talks on the telephone instead, you may need to rewrite the privilege as "use of electronic things." You may have chosen a privilege that is too difficult for the child to earn. In this case, you may want to reward the child with a token, and a certain number of tokens could earn the privilege.

Often, parents write rules about getting better grades in school. If a child is doing poorly, the parents may give the child some privilege if she passes all her subjects in, say, a nine-week grading period. Clearly, this time frame is too long. Rules about schoolwork and grades should be based on day-to-day or weekly issues. In many schools, children get graded on many things during the course of a week: pop quizzes, homework, tests, and the like. In a week, a child can sometimes bring home ten different grades. In this case, it would be highly motivating to earn a reward with each grade.

A child should be required to do a regular amount of homework nightly regardless of whether she has any. This will avoid the issue of whether there is homework or not. The child should show daily that an amount of studying that is normal for her grade level has been completed. Sometimes a child is a slow learner or is not interested in school because of poor teaching. These are more reasons why it is best to make rules about study habits first. See Chapter 4 for more about school motivation.

The list below reviews issues for enforcing rules.

Enforcement of Rules

✔ 100% enforcement is essential—no exceptions, unless the rule has been lifted ahead of time.

✔ If a rule is no longer needed and good behavior is possible without it, stop the rule and praise the child.

✔ Enforce rules unemotionally; ignore arguing and explanations. If you wrote a rule correctly, you should know if it was broken.

✔ Expect testing of the rules. In fact, many children's behavior worsens after starting this program. The child wants you to give it up and will make it tough on you.

✔ Parents must both agree on rules and enforce them equally. This includes all adults living or supervising in the home.

✔ If the child refuses to have a privilege taken away, enforce the contract by physically taking the privilege away.

Now, some final ideas and observations: This program works, in my experience, about 90% of the time. Its failure usually involves a parent who uses it incorrectly or who just gives up. Stick with the program; it can work for you. Sometimes it is helpful for a parent to get support from another parent or from a school guidance counselor. Often, when we are frustrated in trying to do something new, support in the form of talking and airing feelings with someone or getting a friend to use the particular program, too, may be useful in overcoming some of the difficulties. It can make a difference.

In unusual cases, a child's inappropriate behavior may have an emotional illness as its basis. If you suspect that, consult someone you trust such as the family doctor, a minister, or a school guidance counselor. You could also contact a professional who specializes in working with children, such as a mental health counselor, social worker, psychologist, psychiatrist, or pastoral counselor.

Also, it is important to always give praise along with the reward you give your child. Eventually, you may be able to give up the formal rules and privileges and to rely only on the use of praise.

Many children's behavior problems, especially with children aged 2–12, can also be dealt with, at least in part, by using another technique that is highly recommended by professionals. This technique, called "Time Out," is somewhat like sending a child to her room when she misbehaves, but it involves a very, very important difference: Time Out isolates the child for a very short period of time in a very boring, nonrewarding place. The technique also teaches the child not only what was done wrong but also what behavior is correct. It is not just a punishment; it is also a teaching technique. This approach works well with younger children, and you should consult Chapter 3 if you are interested in learning this additional technique.

Finally, in review, on the next page is a list of "must" things that you are going to have to do to make this program successful. Doing them increases the chances that the program will work for you.

Ways to Ensure Success

▷ *Get your child involved in making rules;* ask her what she wants by way of privileges.

▷ As problems arise, you may write new rules, but *always try to think about possible problems ahead of time,* if possible, and write rules about them.

▷ *Once you have completed the Family Contract, type it on a plain piece of paper.* In the adult world, people do business in this formal way, with a typewritten contract, and it is good to begin teaching this to your child.

▷ *You must post the Family Contract on the refrigerator*—a very public place where it can be referred to very easily. This is absolutely essential. If you do not do this, the program will probably not work. Just this minor difference can mean the difference between success and failure. After a rule is broken, always go to the refrigerator in a robotlike way and show the child the consequences on the contract.

▷ *You must enforce rules 100% of the time.*

▷ *Use praise in addition to the earning of a privilege;* that is, use them together.

▷ *Enforce rules unemotionally.* No arguing, yelling, or getting upset. This will take practice and willpower on your part, but it is necessary, and in the long run, it will make discipline much easier for you. When the child breaks a rule, the consequences must be enforced. Let the Family Contract be the "bad guy." This takes a lot of pressure off you, because getting angry at kids, arguing with them, and punishing them take a toll on parents.

▷ *Stick with it; this program can work for you!*

**Rules must be permanently posted in a
"public" place and enforced unemotionally.**

That's the program! Good luck! Remember, in your household, you can be the boss when you have to be. In the long run, you will even make life easier for your child, because you will be setting important limits, and they will be fair limits. The child can have what she wants, if she learns to behave appropriately.

The next chapter is designed to help you explain the program to your child.

Chapter 2
A Chapter for Kids: All About Rules

✍ A Note to Parents

If you use the rule/privilege program discussed in Chapter 1, you may read this chapter to your child to help her understand the program.

This chapter is meant for children and teenagers. Your mother or father or both are about to begin a program at home to help you all get along better. Your parents are responsible for raising you in a way that helps you learn how to behave correctly and become a good adult. Some parents will be using this program because their child or teenager is having problems at home. In many cases, the child or teenager doesn't think there are any problems, but the parents do. They believe there is a problem, and therefore they have decided to use this program to try to help you. In other cases, parents may use this program even when there are not any special problems at home. In this case, the program can still help families get along better, and it may prevent serious problems from developing. So when parents use this program, it doesn't necessarily mean that there are problems. The program is simply to help you get along at home the best you can.

The program is for both parents and their children or teenagers. First, here's why it's meant for parents. Parents sometimes have trouble disciplining their children. Often, when you do something wrong, your parents punish you *afterward*. With a young child, this punishment might be in the form of a spanking or grounding to the house or bedroom. For a teenager, it might be a strong talking-to, a lecture, or being yelled at. Sometimes, a privilege, such as the use of the telephone or a bike, is taken away. These things usually happen *after* you have done something wrong, sometimes after you have already been given a warning. With this kind of punishment there is a big problem for both parents and children. For parents, it is a pretty emotional situation. They are really upset with the way you have behaved. Sometimes, out of frustration, they will give a very big punishment, a very strong one—perhaps grounding for a number of days. Sometimes they might do almost nothing when you may have done exactly the same thing that was punished before. Sometimes they will be in a bad mood and do one thing; at other times, perhaps on your birthday, they won't do anything at all. Obviously, trying to help you with your behavior by punishing you so you'll learn the right way to behave can be difficult for parents. This program is for them because it will help them to help you in a very consistent way. This means that they are always going to react to the same behavior in the same way. With this program, you'll always know how your parents are going to act.

How Will the Program Help You?

Now how is this program for you—a child or teenager? At first thought, you might be upset that your parents are going to try to do something different. However, this program will really make life easier for you. There are going to be some changes, some that you may not like. It may seem a little strict at first. But in fact, this program will help make things consistent so you will always know how your parents are going to act. There will be no more guessing about what your parents will do. Most important, you will always know what is expected of you. Always! And if you don't follow the expected behavior, you will always know what will happen.

So to summarize, this is a program to help you if you are a child or teenager between 5 and 18 years old (or older if the person is still living at home). The program is meant to help your parents as well as you by making things very consistent and predictable: you will always know what to expect of your parents, and they will know what to expect from you. In some cases, you may be having some behavior problems, at least from your parents' point of view. But in other cases, the program will be used even when things are going pretty well at home; your parents might just want to make it easier. In fact, this program works well in any household and should make it easier for both you and your parents to get along together.

What Is This Program?

The next few pages will tell you more about this program, which is called the Rule/Privilege Program. First, let's talk about what both words in that name mean, and then we'll discuss how the program works and what you can expect once you and your parents begin to use it.

A rule, especially a rule about your behavior, means something you are supposed to do or not do. With this program, we are mostly going to talk about things you are supposed to do, things that are expected of you. An example is chores you are supposed to do, perhaps clean up your room or vacuum the house once a week. You might have a curfew to be home at a certain time. Or maybe you are supposed to do homework every night. These are all examples of rules that say you are supposed to do something.

Another type of rule can be about things you are not supposed to do. Fighting and being disrespectful to someone are two examples of things your parents probably don't want you to do. In this program, these kinds of rules will be put in the positive, which means we won't say, "Don't fight," but instead we'll say, "You must get along with your brother and sister without touching each other physically and hurting one another." Of course, this means you are not allowed to hit your brother or sister. But again, we will try to put the rules in a positive way, telling you what you are expected to do.

Next, we come to the word "privilege." What is a privilege? A privilege is something that you earn. This is very important to understand. It is like a reward. You know what the word "reward" means. If you do something good, your parents often reward you for it. Sometimes a reward might be a word of praise: "You did a good job; I'm proud of you." A very specific kind of reward might be getting some tickets to a ball game or getting a new pair of designer jeans. When you have done something well, you are rewarded for it.

The reason this is called the Rule/Privilege Program is that it is based on certain rule-behaviors that you will be required to do. A rule-behavior is simply following a rule with a specific behavior, such as getting home on time. In return for following that rule, you will get a certain privilege. You will always get that privilege free as long as you follow the rule. You will always know ahead of time that if you don't follow the rule, you won't get the privilege. It's as simple as that. It's your choice now. It's okay if you choose that you don't want the privilege; then you don't have to follow the rule. But if you want the privilege, that is, the reward, you do need to follow the rule.

What Have Your Parents Done?

Right now, this might all seem a little confusing. Let's look at what your mother or father or both have done and how it's going to work. That might make it easier to understand.

Your parents have made a list of your behaviors that concern them or ones that they want to expect of you. It might be coming home on time; it might be getting along with your brother or sister; it might be doing your homework or any other kind of behavior. After they wrote down those behaviors, they took the list and picked three or four of the most important ones to make into rules. So you will be expected to follow three or four different rules that they have written.

Next, they made a list of privileges, that is, things that are important to you. They started with a long list and picked three or four of the things that you like most. Some things may not be important to you, but others will be; everybody values something. Some people don't care about watching TV or about getting an allowance, but they may care a lot about having their own telephone or their own bike and being able to talk or ride whenever they want. Your parents have chosen three or four of your favorite privileges to be yours in return for following the rules. One important point here: you are already getting most of these privileges free, and now your mom and dad are going to make you do something before you get them. This might upset you, but remember: you can still get your privileges. In fact, parents often give their children more privileges with this program than they would normally. Of course, they get good behavior in return. So you can get what you want, but now you will be expected to give something in return.

The Reason Privileges Will Not Be Free

Your parents have not been wrong in giving you these privileges free in the past. However, they are starting this program because it provides two basic advantages. The first advantage is that it will help prepare you for adult life. The fact is, in adult life, you don't get a lot of free things. You are usually expected to do something, and in return you get rewarded. Your parents want to help you prepare for adult life, and this will be a good learning experience for you.

The second advantage of this program is that it will make your life much easier. Here's why. Sometimes, when you misbehave, your parents will suddenly take away a privilege. You might get grounded (lose your privilege to leave the house), lose the use of the telephone, lose the use of your bike, or lose the use of the TV. Suddenly, a privilege is taken away—it's gone! You never know what your parents are going to do. Sometimes they do this—sometimes they do that—sometimes they are fair—sometimes they are unfair. Well, this program will make it a lot easier for you, because from now on things will be very predictable. You will always know exactly what's going to happen. So, out of the blue, your parents will not suddenly take away something that is very important to you. You can always have the privileges you want if you follow the rules; it will be up front, and there will never be any question about it.

At this point, you know that your parents have written three or four rules and have made a list of three or four privileges that you can get if you follow the rules. Your parents should talk with you before they write the final rules and privileges. Give them your ideas. This will help make the rules and privileges that everyone wants.

What Is a Family Contract?

Your parents will be writing a Family Contract. A Family Contract is the official written rules and privileges. A contract, as you may know, is a legal paper. You should treat the Family Contract as an important agreement between you and your parents.

The Family Contract is divided into two sides. On the left side is a list of all the rules—three or four or maybe even five. On the right side of the paper are listed the privileges you can have as long as you follow the rules. Every privilege will be paired with a particular rule. This will be very clear. Talk it over with your parents and make sure that everyone agrees on the rules and the privileges.

At the bottom of the Family Contract is a space to write in growth privileges. Growth privileges are simply activities that parents think are very important, such as the 4-H Club, Boy Scouts or Girl Scouts, or athletics such as the school football team. It might also be involvement in the library club or church youth group. Whatever your growth privileges, your parents will always give them to you free—you do not have to earn these. There are some worthwhile activities that parents think children and teenagers should have the right to do, no matter what. You will never have them taken away. Sometimes, your parents may want you to do a growth activity that you don't want to do. They might decide to make it a rule, so you can earn a privilege in return for participating in the activity. The reason they might do this is because they think the activity is important for your growth.

At the very bottom of the Family Contract is space for the date and for everybody in the family to sign it. The contract is to be posted on the refrigerator. It will always be there for you to look at so you can know exactly what is expected of you in order for you to have the privilege that you want.

What Happens If You Don't Follow the Rules?

You can always have the privileges listed on the right side of the page of the Family Contract as long as you follow the rules. If you don't follow the rules, this is what's going to happen: One of your parents will call you over, and the two of you will go to the refrigerator and look at the contract together. You will see what the result is for not following the rule—the loss of a certain privilege. Your parent will explain to you that you have lost that privilege for a period of time and that after that amount of time, you can have the privilege back if you follow the rule then. If you still don't follow the rule, you still won't get the privilege.

This trip to the refrigerator to read the Family Contract is very important and must be taken every time a rule is broken. Your parents know that even if you refuse to go to the refrigerator with them because you are mad, they are required to go to the refrigerator and look at the contract. You should go with them, however, because this is part of the program and it is important for you to learn what is expected and to know what the results are.

Your parents have written the rules in a way to make them enforceable 100% of the time. That means that you can't get away with anything. If you want to test them to see if they will enforce a rule, that's okay. In fact, young people usually do test the rules to see if their parents really mean business. If your parents are going to follow this program, however, they do mean business. They will enforce the rules 100% of the time; break a rule, and you will lose that privilege—guaranteed!

Why the Family Contract Will Make It Easier for You

In the long run, this program will make things much easier for you because there will never be the issue of whether something is fair. The rules will be so clearly written that if you have broken one, it will be clear to everyone that you have broken it, and you will lose your privilege.

Your parents are instructed by this program to enforce the rules in a way that is called "unemotionally." When your parents get mad at you, they might yell or do any number of things, and you might even yell back at them. All of this is unnecessary. In this program they will enforce the rules like a robot, without any emotion. They also have been told not to listen to any arguments from you, to ignore any screaming or carrying on by you. The results of breaking a rule are clearly decided well ahead of time. You know what is expected of you, and you know you have the choice. If you really don't care and don't want the privilege, that's fine; then break the rule. That's up to you; it's your choice.

Again, this program should make your world much easier because you won't have to hassle your parents and spend half your time figuring out what they are going to do and trying to get around a rule. The rules in the Family Contract have no loopholes, and your parents will enforce them every time, so you will know exactly what's what. This makes things easier for everybody.

Let's go back to a point made earlier. It may upset you that your parents are changing things and that now some of your privileges that were free before must be earned by following rules. It is understandable that this might upset you, and you might say that your friend next door doesn't have to do this kind of thing. Just keep in mind another point made earlier—that this program will help you prepare for the adult world. If you look at what is expected of adults, you will see they are required to follow certain rules and to do certain things in life in order to get the privileges they want. That's just the way the adult world is. Adults also use contracts in their lives. Using the Family Contract in this program will help you learn how adults do business in their world. So, yes, this program may be for young people who are having problems or for parents who just want to change the way they are doing things around the house, but it is also a program for mature young people who want to be everything they can be. It is a program to help you grow up to be a better adult.

What If You Don't Like a Rule?

In some cases, your parents may make a rule that you don't like. Remember though, they are your parents and they know what's best for you. You may think a rule is unfair, but you will still have to live with it. Rules do not have to be fair. What is guaranteed to be fair in this program is the enforcement of the rules; it will always be done in the same way. So if you think a rule is unfair, just remember—it will be enforced fairly and you won't have to worry about getting punished in a way that seems unfair.

It is hoped that you will give this program a very good try. It was mentioned earlier that the program may be upsetting at first. You are used to your parents' doing whatever they do now to discipline you, and that may seem safer. At least that seems predictable to you now. You have been following your parents' rules and living with their punishments for a long time now. Having to do something different can be upsetting. So maybe you will test the rules to see if your parents really mean business, to see if they might give up and go back to the way things used to be. This is normal. But once the program gets going and you realize that your parents will enforce the rules and that you will have to live with the rules, then you'll find after a few weeks that it really is easier to follow the rules, because then you can have the privileges you want. Many times you can get more from your parents than you originally did with the old ways they disciplined you. As in many cases in life, you can get most things you want in life if you follow the rules.

Good Luck!

This program is designed to make your life easier. The rules will be enforced fairly, and you will always know what your parents will do for punishment. Be sure to tell your parents the things you really want and the things you are willing to do to get those privileges. You can get an awful lot if you show that you are mature (grown-up) and can follow rules.

Chapter 3
At Your Wits' End:
Punishment with Young Children

No matter how hard we try to encourage our children toward good behavior, there are times when our efforts fail. Most frequently, parents go to professionals for help with their children's misbehavior only after their attempts at punishment no longer work. Exasperated, they seek outside help; they are at their wits' end.

Though child psychologists and other kinds of parent counselors do not have any magic solutions, sometimes they can offer parents important guidance. Most parents do a good job of disciplining their children, using methods that usually work. But when the usual methods fail, and frustration builds, a different approach is called for. Most parents use some form of punishment as part of their discipline program. The purpose of this chapter is to help parents to learn and use a different method of punishment for a child who is not responding to current punishments. But before discussing this different method of punishment, called "Time Out," it will be helpful to outline some background information about punishment and how it works, or doesn't work, to change behavior. Reading the following discussion about punishment will also help you to understand why your child is behaving as he is in response to punishment.

**Physical punishment takes a
greater toll on the parent than on the child!**

Some Background About Punishment

Punishment is intended to decrease the occurrence of misbehavior. It involves either doing something to the child (e.g., spanking) or removing something desired by the child (e.g., an allowance or special privilege).

Punishment is effective only when it occurs immediately after the misbehavior (i.e., don't wait for Father or Mother to come home to give the punishment) and only when it is given consistently after each and every similar misbehavior, rather than only sometimes. It is ineffective to spank a child for teasing his brother only when he is loud and Mom has had a tiring day. Punishment is also effective only when used together with rewards for appropriate behaviors. In other words, punishment alone does not produce new, appropriate behaviors; instead, it teaches only how not to behave. Encouraging good behavior requires rewarding the child when he behaves appropriately.

Unfortunately, punishment, as it is used by many parents, fails without one or more of these essential ingredients: it must be immediate, must be consistent, and must be accompanied by rewards for appropriate behavior. As a result, punishment often does not work well. Here is a list of some of the likely results of *ineffective* punishment:

❑ *When You Stop Punishment*
Quite simply, when the punishment is stopped, the punished behavior often begins again at the same intensity or frequency.

❑ *"When the Cat's Away, the Mice Will Play"*
The child often still misbehaves when the punisher is not present.

❑ *Fear*
The person who gives the punishment becomes seen as the "punisher," and the child may learn to fear the punisher, especially if the child is physically punished. Needless to say, this can significantly hurt the relationship between the child and the person giving the punishment.

❑ *Undesirable Behavioral By-Products*
The educational psychologist Edward Thorndike was the first to observe in his experiments in the early 1900s that punishment does not always have the effect of weakening or eliminating bad behavior in cats. Instead, punishment may increase the *kinds* of behavior, eventually leading to a response that results in something positive to the animal—escaping punishment. Thus, the animal learns a new "escape" behavior without actually "unlearning" the punished behavior. This principle is essential in our understanding of human behavior. In humans, other undesirable behaviors that lessen or avoid punishment often develop, especially if a child receives very frequent or harsh punishment. To cope, the child may develop complex and pre-

dictable behaviors to avoid punishment (for example, lying or running away). Any behavior that successfully reduces or avoids punishment will increase. Lying is probably the most common example of this. As you can see, the side effects of punishment may prove to be worse than the behavior the punishment was meant to stop.

❏ *Aggression*
The punished child may begin to direct aggressive behavior toward the punisher or toward others.

❏ *Other Side Effects*
Emotional or physical side effects can be caused by punishment or the threat of punishment. Bedwetting, nervousness or nervous habits, stomach problems, and headaches are common examples.

❏ *Only Temporary Effectiveness*
Because punishment usually causes a temporary weakening of the unwanted behavior, parents may use it as their major approach to changing a child's behavior. Quite simply, it becomes habit-forming. As a result, some of the most loving parents may resort to punishment with great frequency. Children quickly learn when the punishment is likely or unlikely to occur. It is for this reason that we may hear parents comment: "We spank him when he hits his little brother, but he's always doing it on the sly when he thinks we can't see him."

❏ *Emotional Price Tag*
The use of punishment, especially physical punishment such as spankings, causes emotional hardships for parents. The old expression "this hurts me more than you" is all too true. Whether the punishment is spanking, lecturing, yelling, or scolding, the emotional price tag is very high for parents. Punishment is costly emotionally.

❑ *Imitative Behavior*
Children imitate adult behavior. Imitation is a very powerful form of learning. Physical punishment of children has been shown to cause aggression (that is, physical acting out) and other disruptive emotional responses such as crying and excessive anger. Remember, behavior begets its own kind!

❑ *Reasoning vs. Punishment*
Some parents do not punish their young children often but instead attempt to reason with them, that is, talk it over with them and appeal to their good sense. However, it is important to remember that until about age 12, children do not have the cognitive thinking capacities to use language to control their behavior. Therefore, although talking to the child is a good idea, it is not enough. The child must also experience a consequence for his behavior that will serve as a "reminder" about appropriate and inappropriate behavior. Obviously, there is a great need for a carefully planned approach to using punishment more effectively and more appropriately—a method to replace the often inconsistent, harsh punishment techniques of many parents.

The method of discipline you are about to learn is called "Time Out." It is a mild yet effective form of punishment that almost completely eliminates undesirable side effects.

Who Should Use Time Out?
Time Out is used primarily with children aged 2–12, but it is not suggested for use with every child in this age group. If the discipline methods you use with your child work well, then stick with them. Time Out is meant for situations when other forms of punishment no longer work or when discipline is not as effective as you would like it to be. It most commonly replaces spanking, which is the kind of punishment most parents use with young children. Time Out is a mild form of punishment that is an effective substitute for hitting, spanking, yelling, scolding, and lecturing. These forms of punishment have a high emotional price tag for the parent; Time Out does not, as you will see. Therefore, counselors also recommend the use of Time Out by par-

ents who are afraid they may lose control and possibly abuse their child.

**Physical punishment often leads to
many undesirable behavioral side effects.**

How Effective Is Time Out?

Time Out will work with most children. It is a very, very powerful technique, and therein lies the problem. If used correctly, Time Out almost always results in a decrease in the problem behavior. However, the incorrect use of Time Out can cause problem behaviors to increase. When Time Out is unsuccessful, it is usually because the parent has failed to use the technique correctly. If necessary, get help from a professional child counselor who can give you the extra support you may need to make the technique work for you.

Defining the Behavior You Want to Change

Often, when parents have reached their wits' end and are desperate to try a new approach, they have a long list of misbehaviors that must be changed. Nevertheless, for best results, you should begin Time Out with only a few behaviors. First, allow the technique to succeed, and then slowly expand its use to other behaviors. You will have to begin with only a few problem behaviors—the ones most important to you. Make a list on the next page of all the behaviors you are concerned about. Be specific. For example, instead of listing "poor attitude," list all the behaviors that are examples of "poor attitude."

List of Problem Behaviors

Example: *He teases his little brother.*

1.

2.

3.

4.

5.

6.

7.

8.

**Yelling may let off some steam, but
it has an emotional price tag for you.**

When to Use Time Out

Now that you have made a list of all of your child's problem behaviors, you must choose the behaviors to start using Time Out on. First, choose only two or three; you can use Time Out on more behaviors once the approach is working well for you. Choose only frequent behaviors—ones that happen often during the day, not only once in a while. "Whining" and "not obeying a command" are typical examples of frequent problem behaviors, whereas "fighting with a sibling" may occur only once or twice a week. Although fighting is a very important problem behavior, and you can use Time Out as a punisher for it, it is important to begin the Time Out method with behaviors that occur often enough for the child to experience the consequence of Time Out often. This will help him learn appropriate behavior more rapidly. Of course, if fighting occurs frequently, you may certainly use it to start the program.

Some behaviors are more easily dealt with using the rule/privilege method described in "Rules for Unruly Children" (Chapter 1). Typically, a rule/privilege program is used in addition to Time Out with young children, especially aged 7–12. The rule/privilege program is also the major disciplinary approach to working with teenagers. After you have successfully begun Time Out, read Chapter 1 (if you haven't already), which describes how to use a rule/privilege program with your child.

One other suggestion: To begin a Time Out program, you might want to choose frequent problem behaviors that are especially irritating to you. That way, when you decrease the behaviors, you will be reducing the emotional price tag for yourself.

The reason for writing down your child's problem behaviors, rather than just thinking about them, is to begin to practice an essential part of the Time Out method. The Time Out consequence must also be set out in advance and written down. When you have decided on the two or three problem behaviors to begin using Time Out on, write them down on a piece of paper, and post it on your refrigerator at a height your child can easily see. The importance of this step will become clear later.

Make Your Rules Specific

Probably the biggest mistake parents make when describing problem behaviors is being too general. A stranger should be able to enter your home, read the Time Out rules on your refrigerator, and enforce them. There should never be any question of whether or not a rule has been broken. Look at the sample rule on the next page and then write your own, being as specific as possible.

Bad Time Out Rule	Good Time Out Rule
1. No talking back to your mother or father.	1. When unhappy about what Mother or Father is doing, talk in a normal voice (not loudly), and don't whine or cry. Do not show you're upset by throwing things, slamming doors, pounding on the floor or wall, cursing, or hitting."

Time Out Rules

Write your Time Out rules here.

1.

2.

3.

Final Time Out Rules

Now rewrite the rules here, trying to be even more specific. There is a purpose to it. As you will soon see, not only is Time Out not only a form of punishment, but it also stresses teaching correct behavior. So try to write your rules in the positive, that is, not "Don't do _____," but rather "Do _____."

1.

2.

3.

Post the Rules

Now that you have the Time Out rules fine-tuned, write them on the official rule form on the next page, and post them on the refrigerator. Fill in the child's name at the top. Use a separate sheet for each child you plan to use Time Out with. If the rules are exactly the same for two or more children, then put both their names on one sheet. You will note that there is a place for your child to sign the form, a place for parents to sign, and a place for others to sign (e.g., a baby-sitter or a grandparent living in the home. Sign the form when you teach Time Out to your child, which you will soon learn to do. Now it is time to talk about how to use Time Out.

Time Out rules must be permanently written down.

Time Out Rules

Child's Name:

1.

2.

3.

_____   _____
Child's Signature   Parent's Signature

_____   _____
Other's Signature   Parent's Signature

"Grounding" or Sending Your Child to His Room

When I was growing up, my father often disciplined me by sending me to my room. I was told to go to my room and stay there until allowed to come out. Sometimes I was told to think about how bad I had acted, while "doing time" in my room. Interestingly, I don't recall that this form of punishment, or "grounding" as it was called, had much of an effect on me. I usually passed my time listening to the radio (with an earphone), gazing out the window at the activity on the street, or working on my rock collection. When time was up, I came from the room looking troubled and saying I would now behave myself.

"Grounding" can be a useful form of punishment, since it attempts to bring an undesirable consequence to a misbehavior, usually in the form of taking away a child's freedom to do desirable activities. However, parents often make the mistake of sending a child to his room when misbehavior occurs; they forget that the room is full of desirable things such as toys, radios, and books.

You Say "I've Already Tried That"

When I describe Time Out as very much like sending a child to his room, most parents say, "I've already tried that. I've tried standing him in a corner or sending him to his room, and it doesn't work." Usually, when asked about the specific grounding method they used, the parents admit that they did not send the child every time he performed the misbehavior and that the room had many desirable things to do. Standing a child in a corner doesn't work for this same reason; he can hear interesting things or sneak a look over his shoulder and see interesting things. This is *not* Time Out! Time Out must be used with 100% consistency, and it must be carried out in a place that is very unrewarding, uninteresting, dull, and boring. That's where the name comes from: *Time Out* from all rewarding things. So, Time Out differs in several ways from sending a child to his room. Most parents send a child to his room for long periods of time, ranging from 30 minutes to all day. Time Out is different, and these differences are important. Time Out puts a child in a totally nonrewarding place for a very short period of time. The way you enforce it—unemotionally—is critical also. So, if you say you have already tried sending your child to his room and it doesn't work, that's not Time Out. Read on.

**Sending a child to his room
may not be much of a punishment.**

Where to Time Out Your Child

Every time your child breaks a Time Out rule, he is to go to the Time Out place. Remember, the best characteristic of the place for Time Out is that it should be very dull. My experience and the experience of many parents and child counselors point to the bathroom as the best such place. There should be no toys, TV, books, or people. in the bathroom. The child may play with the water at first, but don't worry, this interest will pass. If you want, you can turn off the water under the sink (most children have not discovered the turnoff valve there). If the child does make a mess with the water, then there are ways to handle that, which we'll discuss later.

You should childproof the bathroom before using it for Time Out. Remove all but essential things, and lock closets and cabinets if possible. If the child is likely to get into things, then you may want to use a plastic bucket to put your toilet articles in. Simply remove the bucket when using Time Out. This is a bit bothersome, yes, but it is worth it if you are highly motivated to get your child's behavior under control.

When you put your child in Time Out, you will be shutting the door. Don't worry about the Department of Social Services coming to investigate you for child abuse, but do make sure the room has plenty of air and lighting. Also, plan an emergency fire escape route ahead of time. As you will see next, Time Out is not like flinging your child into a dungeon and throwing away the key; in fact, he will be there only a very short time.

How Long Should a Child Be in Time Out?

Research on the use of Time Out has shown that 3–5 minutes of Time Out is as effective as 20–30 minutes of Time Out. Therefore, use 3 minutes for very young children (2–5 years old) and 5 minutes for older children. As you will see later, it will be possible to add a little time to the Time Out penalty if necessary. However, as a general rule of thumb, 1 minute of Time Out may be used for each year of age of the child. Use a portable-type kitchen timer, and set it for the penalty time when the child goes into Time Out. Then both the child and parent will know by a clear signal when Time Out is over.

Time Out Is Punishment Plus Teaching

Time Out is an effective form of punishment if it is used as punishment should be—consistently. It works by a "conditioning process," in which the misbehavior and the penalty are paired together many times. The effect of these many pairings is that the child decreases the misbehavior to avoid the penalty. But punishment tells the child only what not to do. Time Out goes further, because it also involves teaching the child proper behavior. It serves as a reminder of how to behave correctly. You may doubt that the child experiences punishment as a simple reminder, but again, this is how Time Out is different.

The bathroom is often the best place to Time Out a child.

As you will see, you are to enforce Time Out unemotionally. One purpose of unemotional enforcement is to decrease your emotional burden when you discipline. The other reason for being unemotional is so the child is not emotionally hurt or offended. Then, the child is free to serve his time and view Time Out as a reminder, not as a heavy-handed kind of guilt trip. Furthermore, your child will be more open to learning the behavior lesson if emotions are not involved.

When your child breaks a Time Out rule, you are to inform him that he has broken a rule and take him immediately to the refrigerator. There, you simply read the rule and point out that the *reminder* (you should use that word) is 5 minutes (or whatever period) in Time Out. This routine will make for the conditioning aspect of Time Out; it follows every occurrence of misbehavior on the Time Out rule list. Conditioning occurs when you do something over and over again, until it becomes second nature.

When the child comes out of Time Out, you should return to the refrigerator and have him read the rule. If he will not read it (or isn't old enough to read), don't make an issue of it; simply read the rule and tell him the consequence. For example, "Johnny, the rule is no teasing your little brother, and every time you do it, you will go to Time Out. Understand?" It is hoped that the child will acknowledge understanding, but if not, don't force the issue. Ask the child to repeat the rule and consequence again. If he won't, again, don't force the issue. If the child will repeat it as requested, say "Thank you" when he finishes. Now is the time to teach. Tell the child what he could have done, that is, explain an appropriate behavior that would have kept him from going into Time Out. For example, "Johnny, you were playing with your brother and wanted to have fun. You could have played a game or looked at your rock collection together. Those behaviors are correct. Having fun by teasing is incorrect. Now, you tell me how you could have behaved correctly." Note this last part: have the child say a correct behavior. Praise the child if he does this, and again, don't force the issue if the child is angry and won't say it. Simply tell the child another example of correct behavior yourself.

The above steps have to be carried out every time the child is put into Time Out. That's right, every time! Now you are beginning to see the important differences between Time Out and methods that seem to be like it; Time Out takes more work by the parent, but that is also why it pays off. In the end, it works!

One final issue here: If the child's misbehavior is something he can still do (e.g., pick up toys) after he comes out of Time Out, you are to take him from the refrigerator back to the scene of the crime. Repeat your command to pick up the toys. Of course, if the child still will not follow the rule, then the whole process starts all over again and the child goes back into Time Out. The purpose here is to get the child to show that he can use the correct behavior you just taught him.

Preparing to Use Time Out

Once you have posted your Time Out rules on the refrigerator, the next step is to practice them with your child. The use of Time Out takes a lot of skill. On the surface, it appears simple: put your child in the bathroom for a short time every time he misbehaves. But as you are discovering, it's the little things about using it that are difficult and that make all the difference in the world. Therefore, the use of Time Out should be discussed beforehand with your child, using a dress rehearsal, so that you are sure about it when you use Time Out the first time.

Explain to your child what will happen when he breaks a Time Out rule. Then, pretend he broke one. Go through each step of Time Out, explaining to your child along the way. However, when just practicing, don't make him stay in Time Out for longer than 15 seconds while at the same time explaining the real consequence. I suggest that you practice Time Out at least twice before starting it.

You may wish to use a warning to indicate to the child that he is about to break a Time Out rule. But remember, once a rule is broken, Time Out must be enforced. So be sure to use a warning only before the rule is broken. As an example, if the child has been told to pick up his toys and he doesn't, you may warn him: "If you don't pick up your toys in 5 seconds, you have broken the rule about following directions and you will go into Time Out." Or, a pre–Time Out warning signal can tell the child that he must stop the behavior immediately or go into Time Out. A nonverbal signal, such as the hand signal used by football officials to call time out, shown in the picture on the next page, is useful in avoiding arguments and complaints by the child.

**A hand signal may be used
to warn a child about Time Out.**

Enforcing Time Out

There are two basic rules about enforcing Time Out: (1) be consistent, and (2) do it unemotionally—"be a robot."

We have already discussed the issue of consistency and how important it is to the success of the program. You must enforce the Time Out procedure every time the child breaks a Time Out rule. No exceptions!

And second, when you Time Out your child, be calm. Do not scold or nag. Do not engage in an argument about the broken rule. Be very firm. Ignore any squabbling. Be a robot—no emotions. Channel your energy into doing the method correctly, step by step, rather than spending it on getting upset. Do not raise your voice or allow any body language or facial expressions to show dislike, disappointment, or the like. Simply remind the child that he broke a Time Out rule, and then go ahead and enforce it. This part of enforcement is very important, so if you're having trouble with it, practice with a friend or spouse. Practice it again and again until it becomes natural.

Who Enforces Time Out?

Time Out must be used every time the problem behavior occurs. Both parents and all adult members of the household must help in using Time Out. If your child spends a great deal of time at, for example, the grandparents' house, you should ask for their help there. Teach them the method, and be sure it is enforced. In this case, grandparents are not for spoiling!

Later, we will talk about how to use Time Out when you're away from home, such as in the car or at the store.

What Happens When You Start to Use Time Out?

Unfortunately, many parents give up on the Time Out technique very soon after starting it, claiming, "It doesn't work; my child's behavior got worse." Right! You can expect that. Many instances of Time Out will be necessary before you see a positive change. Don't give up. Your early efforts will be worth it in the long run. No human being likes to have his behavior changed. We like to be able to predict what will happen to us. Though your child might have been getting spanked before you started to use Time Out, at least that was predictable. Time Out is something new, and it will take a while for the child to get used to it and for it to become predictable for him. Often, the child's worsening behavior is an attempt to get you to give up Time Out and to go back to the old methods. And many children succeed: the parents give up. However, if you stick with it, after you consistently use Time Out for a few weeks, the child's misbehavior will begin to decrease.

Even after Time Out begins to work, your child's problem behavior will not just disappear forever; rather, you can expect it to appear again from time to time. This, again, is predictable. It's called "testing behavior" and it's normal for a child experiencing a change in behavior. Do not view it as a sign of failure; be assured that things are going normally, and continue to enforce Time Out firmly and consistently.

What Ifs

What ifs are common problems that arise when you use Time Out. Typically, parents wonder, "Well, what if the child . . . ?" Here are some ways of handling those situations.

❑ *Child Won't Go to Time Out.* If the child will not go to Time Out, tell him that if he does not go to Time Out immediately, you will add 1 extra minute to the Time Out period. You can continue with that plan, 1 minute at a time, up to about 10 minutes. If the child still refuses to go to Time Out, then inform the child that if he does not go to Time Out in the next 10 seconds, TV privileges will be lost for that night (or dessert, or the use of the bicycle, or the right to leave the yard to play). Then, leave the area. If the child does not go to Time Out within 10 seconds, then enforce the backup consequence immediately—on that very day. You do have another option, but it works only for unique situations. If the child is small and you can physically force him into Time Out without getting into a knock-down-drag-out fight, then you may calmly state to the child that if he does not go to Time Out on his own, you will carry him there. It's his choice. The problem with this option is that it may renew the emotional price tag for the parent, though for some, it is possible to do with little emotional involvement.

❑ *Child Won't Stay in Time Out.* If the child will not stay in the Time Out area or comes out before the time is up, use the same plan as above. As a last resort, you might change the lock on the door. Unfortunately, bathrooms usually lock from the inside. However, it is often a fairly simple task to turn around the door handle yourself. If you are not good at fixing things, a locksmith will do it for about $15. The effort is worth it if you have a child who is "pulling out all the stops" to overthrow your Time Out program.

❑ *Child Is Destructive While in Time Out.* If the child destroys anything in the room during Time Out, then naturally he must pay for it out of his allowance. If the child has messed up the bathroom, he must clean it up before being allowed to leave Time Out. Although it will be difficult, it is important to remain unemotional, even if your child is destructive.

❑ *Child Is Noisy While in Time Out.* The child should not be allowed to leave Time Out until he has stopped crying, kicking, howling, yelling insults, or pounding the door. He must be quiet for at least the last 30 seconds in order to earn release from Time Out. For example, if the child is in Time Out for 5 minutes, he must be quiet from 4 minutes 30 seconds to 5 minutes. If the child has not been quiet during that time, then he must continue in Time Out until 30 seconds in a row of quiet have been completed.

❑ *Child Won't Leave Time Out.* Once the child has completed Time Out, it is the child's own business if he wishes to stay there. This is not an unusual way children behave to try to get your goat. Ignore it and go about your business.

❑ *Child Says He Likes Time Out.* If the child has learned to be a good manipulator, he may say something like "Go ahead; put me in Time Out; I don't care; I like it there." Or perhaps the child acts unaffected by the method after you have used it for a while. Don't worry and don't be fooled. Ignore it and keep up the good work.

Using Time Out Away from Home

Using Time Out away from home is not as difficult as you might think. No, the answer is not to find another place instead of the bathroom. Rather, it's as simple as "marking Time Out." When the child breaks a Time Out rule in the car or at the store or at a friend's house (or possibly even at Grandma's house, if the child visits there only occasionally, or if Grandma is not able to follow through with Time Out), then he is told that he has earned a Time Out. His hand can be marked with a nontoxic, felt-tipped pen to show the number of Time Out periods he must complete later at home: one mark for each broken rule. Then, as soon as you arrive home, place the child into Time Out. If he has several Time Outs to serve, space them out over several hours.

This method of marking Time Out should be practiced at least once before you use it. A good time to do so would be when you teach your child about the general Time Out method. As with the other practice sessions, run through each step, including going somewhere and "pretending" the child has broken a specific Time Out rule. This may seem silly, but it's not. In fact, it's the reason so many parents fail at using Time Out. They don't stick to every step of the plan. So, again, do it. It will make a difference.

If Time Out Fails

There are several options you should consider if Time Out isn't working after a month of consistent use. It's possible that you still may not be doing it correctly. Find someone to support you in your efforts: a friend, a minister, or even a professional child counselor. Often, just having someone there to give you support can make the difference. You can call your support person regularly to report in on how it's going.

Sometimes a child's behaviors don't change because they may be the result of very powerful influences in the child's life. For example, sexual molestation can have very deep and lasting effects. It is best to consult a professional child counselor if misbehavior persists. With such help, you can back off and look at the situation from another point of view. If a behavior will not change with a good solid effort at using Time Out, then it tells us we must look deeper for causes. Seek out a teacher, school counselor, minister, social worker (at your local social services or family services office), mental health counselor, or private counselor. You and your child can be helped.

Time Out may be used away from home.

Review: Key Ideas About Time Out

If this list of guidelines is used, you have an excellent chance of decreasing or eliminating your child's inappropriate behavior through the use of Time Out.

✔ "Time Out" means time out from all rewarding things.

✔ Physical punishment carries an emotional price tag for both the parent and the child.

✔ Time Out is punishment, but with emphasis on teaching the child more appropriate behaviors.

✔ Before using Time Out:
  • Identify frequently occurring problem behaviors.

  • Explain the procedure to the child.

✔ To use Time Out effectively:
  • Parents must be consistent, applying Time Out unemotionally even if the child complains, resists, or promises to stop the misbehavior.

  • A very dull place must be used for Time Out, preferably the bathroom.

  • Use a short period of Time Out, generally no more than 1 minute for each year of the child's age.

  • Both parents and anyone else in charge of the child should use Time Out together.

✔ The child must be verbally rewarded (praised) for good behavior. With Time Out you are giving your attention to problem behavior; therefore, it is important that you also notice and comment on good behavior.

Chapter 4
Whatever Became of Deportment?
Motivating Children and Teenagers
in School

When I was a child, deportment was always a grade on my report card. "Deportment" referred to a student's behavior in school. It no longer appears on most of today's report cards.

For many parents, their child's school performance is a source of much concern and unhappiness. Poor performance can take many forms: disruptive behavior, suspensions, poor attitude, lack of motivation, failure to do homework, performance below ability, and the list goes on. When such behavior occurs, parents find it difficult to stand on the sidelines without trying to do something. Almost all parents know the value and importance of a good education; they want better lives for their children, and education is the best road to it. This special concern with a child's school performance can lead to much worry and frustration if the child is not "making it" in school.

This chapter is meant to help you help your child in school. It puts deportment back on the report card. The approach you will learn to use is not a magic solution, but it does work. Parents use many different ways to encourage their children toward positive school performance. If a method works, and it is not harmful to the child, then fine! But this chapter is for parents who have tried unsuccessfully to change their child's school behavior. The chapter offers a very specific method to help you if you are one of these frustrated parents.

Daily Report Card

The key to your child's improvement in school is the use of a daily report card. Just as it sounds, it's a report that the child gets every day. In most schools, children receive a report card about every nine weeks. When a child receives poor grades or comments about poor behavior on her report card, parents often punish the child by taking away her privileges, "bawling her out," spanking her, and the like. Often, teachers and school officials have already tried to help the child perform better. Unfortunately, the school has little clout to encourage the child to do better. The punishments the school can use for misbehavior are often ineffective. Suspension may get the child right where she wants—out of school. And a poor report card is seldom a useful motivator for school improvement, even if the child is punished for it at home.

Schools and parents usually fail in changing a child's behavior for two major reasons. First, children must have immediate feedback on their behavior/performance. Every nine weeks is just not frequent enough for those who are having school problems. Even one week is too long! Second, children usually have little ongoing responsibility for their behavior at school. They are responsible at school, but as already mentioned, the school's methods to control behavior often are not very effective with problem children. The school's hands are tied. Schools can do only so much. Children need to be held more responsible at home for their school behavior.

The daily report card overcomes these two major hurdles to school success. It provides immediate, daily feedback for the child and parents about the child's behavior in school. Along with the rule/privilege contract, it makes the child responsible for her school behavior/performance at home every day.

Capable children often need to be motivated to perform to their ability.

Rule/Privilege Program

The daily report card is used as part of a rule/privilege program. This method is explained here very briefly; however, you should look at a more complete discussion of it in Chapter 1, "Rules for Unruly Children."

Parents most often discipline their children by taking away some privilege when the child misbehaves. The privilege is usually something highly desired by the child, such as TV time, use of a bike, or freedom to leave the home for activities. An outline of this method would look like the diagram below.

Typical Discipline Program

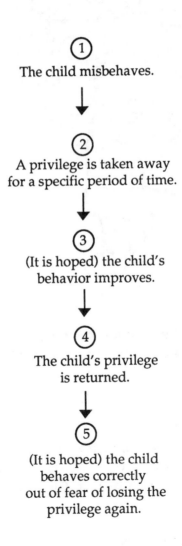

①
The child misbehaves.

②
A privilege is taken away
for a specific period of time.

③
(It is hoped) the child's
behavior improves.

④
The child's privilege
is returned.

⑤
(It is hoped) the child
behaves correctly
out of fear of losing the
privilege again.

This method works well with many children. But, again, you would not be reading this if such methods worked for you. The rule/privilege program is often effective when other approaches are failing. The idea is very simple. You might think of this program as being the opposite of the method just outlined. It looks like this:

Rule/Privilege Discipline Program

Take away all of
the child's major,
desired privileges.

The child behaves
correctly.

The child earns a
desired privilege.

The child does not
behave correctly.

The child does not
earn a desired privilege.

The reason this approach is called a rule/privilege program is that the expected, appropriate behavior you want from the child is set out in the form of a rule. If she follows the rule, she earns the privilege; if she does not follow the rule, she does not get the privilege. Therefore, the program stresses rewards for good behavior. However, it is not like many reward programs, because the rewards are not extra goodies. Instead, they are the privileges the child was often getting free before the program began. The program is also different because it takes much of the discipline out of the parents' hands and puts the responsibility for appropriate behavior on the child, because all the rules and consequences are clearly set out ahead of time. Discipline becomes a task of simply enforcing the rules. If you consult the chapter "Rules for Unruly Children" (Chapter 1), you will see that the rule/privilege program is usually set out in the form of a Family Contract, posted on the refrigerator. Rules must be very specific, and parents must enforce them unemotionally. Rules can include any behaviors, and of course, the ones we are interested in now are school behaviors. A sample rule/privilege contract, using the daily report card, is provided on the next page.

Family Contract

Post on Refrigerator

Rule	Privilege
1. On every school day you must bring home a good report card. ("Good" is defined as no more than two Nos).	1. You may watch TV or use any electronic things (radio, Nintendo, stereo, home computer; includes battery operated) from the time Mom or Dad comes home on school days.

Date _____

Signatures _____ _____

In the sample on the previous page, the daily report card serves as a ticket to watch TV or to have other privileges. Notice that the rule has been carefully written to include what "good" means. The privilege is also written out in a very specific way. Because in this household it appears the child may be home alone with a brother or sister for a while after school, the privilege begins when a parent is there to enforce it. In this case, even when she gets a poor daily report card, the child may watch "Teenage Mutant Ninja Turtles" after school, but as soon as Mom or Dad comes home, the rule is in effect.

This sample should give you a better idea of how the daily report card works within the rule/privilege program. Again, I suggest that you also read Chapter 1.

Involving Your Child's Teacher

In order for you to use a daily report card with your child, you must get the cooperation of her teacher (or teachers). Do not take this for granted! Teachers are busy people. You should respect their time by asking for their help. Teachers are almost always willing to help if you do two things: First, ask them at a time when they are not rushed or stressed. Second, explain the entire program to them. Although their involvement is important, it is also minimal; but by sharing the reasons and plans of your program, you will help them understand their role in it. A successful program may also make their job with your child easier. Should a teacher be uncertain or appear to have it in for your child, ask her to try it for two weeks, and then judge it at that point. Always give the teacher as much feedback as possible about how the program is working. The more a teacher feels a part of the effort and the success of the program, the more the teacher's support and cooperation will be there. A simple letter to the teacher saying how your child's behavior/grades have improved will be appreciated.

You will be asking the teacher (or each teacher) to take about 10 seconds at the end of your child's class to check her daily report card. The teacher is not responsible for keeping the daily note, nor for reminding the child to have it checked. Those two tasks are your child's responsibility.

If it can be arranged, a face-to-face meeting with your child's teacher would be a good way to introduce your program. However, if a meeting is not convenient, a letter will serve the purpose; a sample letter is provided for you on the next page. You should send the letter to the teacher, with a copy of the daily report card, and then follow it up with a phone call a day or two later. This brings us to the next issue: using the daily report card with your child.

Stay in touch with your child's teacher.

Dear _____:

    I would like to ask for your assistance in our attempt to help our child at school. As you know, our child has had some behavior/academic difficulties in school. At home, we are using a rule/privilege program, in which our child can earn favorite privileges after following specific rules. If our child doesn't follow the rules, then the child automatically doesn't get a favorite privilege. I would like to use our home program to make our child more accountable for daily school performance. Therefore, I need daily information from you about our child's performance.

    I have attached a copy of a daily report card. This card is a way for me to know how our child does in school every day. Please let me know if you think the card needs any changes. I need your help in checking Yes or No for each item on the card at the end of our child's class. It usually takes about 10 seconds. While this seems like a small amount of time, I fully realize that class dismissal time is hectic. I know that having a child come to you at that time every day is a nuisance, especially if the other children come to you at that time also, but I really believe this will help our child, and I know you want all your students performing to their capabilities.

    You do not have to worry about having a card each day or even about reminding our child to have you check the card at the end of the class; both tasks are the child's responsibility. I would ask that you complete the card without commenting on poor behavior/academics; simply check the No column. If you like, you may provide extra feedback or praise on any Yes response. If our child argues about any of your judgments, just ignore it please and give her the card after you complete it.

    Please call me if you have any questions. A good time to reach me is _____, at telephone number _____. Thank you.

(signature) _____

How to Use the Daily Report Card

Before you begin to use the daily report card with your child, you should have completed two major steps:

❑ Make a rule/privilege Family Contract with the rule, meaning the expected appropriate behavior, being "bringing home a good report card." Chapter 1 will help you pick out a particular privilege for your child and put it into the contract. Your child will then have to earn the privilege on a daily basis, and her ticket will be a good report card. By the way, the privilege you choose for this program should be one she would like every day. This is because the child must have an immediate consequence for her misbehavior. However, in some cases, when a nondaily privilege is very much enjoyed, it may also work well. For example, if your teenage daughter lives for the chance to date on Friday or Saturday night, you might require four good report cards each week in order to earn that privilege.

❑ Contact the child's teachers and ask for their cooperation.

If you have completed these two steps, you are ready for the next step—beginning the program. Choose the report card you would like to use. There are samples later in this chapter. Feel free to make your own or to modify the samples by changing/adding/subtracting categories. Then make about 50 copies of the daily report card, if possible, on colored paper. (Using colored paper will help your child keep track of these report cards among all her school papers.)

It is time to explain the program to your child. You should read through Chapter 2 with your child or teenager. It will be useful to explain the program purpose to the child. Post the rule/privilege contract on your refrigerator and explain to your child that she will have the desired privilege whenever she gives you a good report card. It is best to start the program in one class only—one of the child's better classes. It is helpful to start out making certain the program succeeds by having the child see that it will be easy to earn her privileges. Therefore, you should contact only one teacher to start the program. Then, after two to three weeks, when things are going well, start the program in another class, and so on every week or two until all of your child's teachers are involved. You can ask the first teacher to talk with the other teachers about the program, thereby saving yourself much time. Of course, if your child is in elementary school and has only one teacher, then this will not be an issue. It is usually good to begin the program by allowing a child two Nos, but no more, and still have a good report card. Then you can change it to one No after all classes have been added. If your child is doing almost nothing right in school, you may want to begin by requiring only two Yeses for a good report card. Start at whatever level will help the child experience success easily at first. This is better than having her get discouraged and give up.

Give your child a stack of the daily report cards, and tell her it is her responsibility to both take one to school each day and give it to the teacher(s) at the end of the class period.

One final point here about starting the program. As suggested in "Rules for Unruly Children" (Chapter 1), it may prove very helpful to get your child's ideas about the best kinds of privileges. Parents usually have a pretty good idea of their child's most desired privileges, but sometimes you can discover very good rewards by asking the child herself. Sometimes she will be willing to follow a difficult rule if, in return, she gets a special reward. However, you must remember not to use growth privileges for this purpose. For example, your child should always be allowed to play in her school volleyball games. Growth privileges must always remain "free." Consult "Rules for Unruly Children" for more about growth privileges. That's all. You're ready to start the program. We will cover other issues when we talk about enforcement later.

Rewarding Good Grades

You have probably noticed that so far nothing has been said about using the rule/privilege program to require better grades, that is, making better grades the rule. That's because the program stresses better school behavior and homework behavior, and usually, improvement in these two areas is enough to cause better grades. In order to help that happen, however, you can set up a separate small reward program for the good grades your child gets. First, set a fair standard for your child, perhaps one letter grade above her average. If the school uses traditional grades, you might choose a B– if she is a C– student. If the school uses percentages (0–100%), you might pick 80 if she normally gets low 70s. Then, you simply tell the child that every mark of 80 or above that she brings to you may be cashed in for a specific reward. For example, if your child should receive about a $2 allowance each week, you might use the rule/privilege program for her to earn the first dollar. Then tell her that for every 80 or above grade she brings to you each Friday night, she can earn 50¢. Usually, children earn many "grades" during the course of a week, so this will give the child plenty of motivation to do well. Of course, you may choose any kind of reward, but experience shows that money works well. You may want to call your child's teacher(s) to get an idea of how many grades she receives during a typical week, such as for homework, quizzes, tests, papers, and book reports. It is best to set the grade goal a little low at first, so the child has immediate success. For example, if she is an all-D and all-F student, don't choose B as your standard; choose C–. Once the child meets your standard with most of her marks each week, you can raise the standard, but only in small steps. By the way, be careful about the size of the reward. One parent who tried this method owed his 10-year-old child $80 after three weeks. Obviously, he had offered too great a reward for each good mark.

As with the rule/privilege program, write down the specifics of this reward program after you have discussed it with your child, and post it on the refrigerator.

Homework: A Special Problem

Homework can be an especially emotional issue for many parents and children. Perhaps the child doesn't do it. Or she says she doesn't have any homework (when she really does). Or she puts it off and always leaves it until the last minute. Or she doesn't spend enough time doing it. Or she always needs help with her homework . . . and so on and so on.

Here's a way to attack this problem that usually works. Choose a very important privilege, one the child enjoys every day. Then, as part of your rule/privilege program, make a rule that your child must complete at least 30 minutes (or whatever the usual amount for a student your child's age) of homework before having the privilege. It's a good idea to have your child study in the same place every day. Create a nice study area, if possible, one free from noise and other people. The "no-homework" problem is avoided by requiring homework, regardless. You can take a large box and put it in the child's study area, filling it with educational materials: math workbooks, *National Geographics* or other educational magazines, books, educational cassette tapes. If your child says she has no homework, she still must obey the rule and complete the required homework time, using materials from the box, if she wants the privilege for that day. Depending on the child, different amounts of checking the completed homework may be necessary. You may have to have her bring you the homework for "approval" before she is given the privilege. In other cases, little checking may be necessary.

The discipline you teach your child with the homework rule will go a long way toward helping her discipline her time for important tasks in her life. The rule may seem strict, but your child will be helped for the rest of her life because of it. A common homework rule is outlined below for you. Note that the rule applies only to school nights.

Rule	Privilege
You must complete 1 hour of homework in your study area, with no distractions (radio, friends, etc.), every school night, to be checked before gaining the privilege.	You may use electronic things on school nights (radio, TV, telephone, Nintendo).

**It is the child's responsibility to give
the daily report card to the teacher.**

How to Enforce the Daily Report Card

As already suggested, this program will discipline your child automatically. However, to make it work, you must see that the consequences set out beforehand are enforced consistently and unemotionally. If your child forgets to take a daily report card to school or loses it, it is no skin off your teeth. In both cases, the child will not present you with a report card, which is the same as all Nos. Because of this, the child does not get the privilege that night. Again, the report card is a ticket to be used to get the privilege. No ticket, no privilege. It's that simple. You have not taken away the privilege; the child simply did not earn it.

Another important point in the enforcement of this rule: you should not ask your child for the report card. It is her responsibility to bring it to you to check. Until she does bring it to you, no privilege. When it is given to you, look at the daily card carefully, looking for any successes you can comment about. For example, "Jenny, I know you have had a difficult time in Mr. Smith's class. You don't like science, and you sometimes feel Mr. Smith is unfair to you. Today you had all Yeses in his class. Congratulations! What did you do to help you to be successful today?" This kind of remark will help your child better understand her behavioral coping skills; she will be more likely to use them in the future if her successes are noticed and praised. After you have reviewed the card, if it is a good report for the day, praise the child for the success and tell her the privilege has been earned.

If the child has a bad report card, just inform her the privilege has not been earned for that day. That's all. Nothing else, unless you want to comment on some success on the card. If she argues or tries to explain how unfair a teacher was or the like, ignore her and repeat the consequence. If she ever tries to use the privilege even when she has not earned it, physically prevent it. See "Rules for Unruly Children" for more about these situations.

You must be very consistent in enforcing the daily report card rule, and you must do so unemotionally. Put your emotional energy into enforcing the program exactly as it has been outlined here rather than getting upset. Showing anger may cause the program to fail. Be a robot. Simply state the consequences to your child. Do not raise your voice, and do not put down the child or appear upset. A fact is a fact. Simply state it; that is all.

If you have already looked at "Rules for Unruly Children," you have seen the warning that a child's behavior will often get worse when you try to change her behavior using a new method. Expect it. Don't give up. If your child makes a fuss about the daily report card, consider yourself on the right track. Stick with it and get some support from others (a friend or the school's guidance counselor) to help you through, if necessary.

If your child appears unaffected by not earning the selected privilege, she may be bluffing. Don't fall for it. After a few weeks, if she continues to be unconcerned, then you should consider whether you have
chosen a little-desired privilege. Or perhaps you started the program by
demanding too much with your rule. In both cases, you can make
changes in the program and continue.

One final point: You and your child should go to the refrigerator
each time you allow a privilege or do not allow it, depending on the results of the daily report card. Look at the Family Contract and repeat the
consequences, good or bad. This may appear to be a waste of your time,
but it is the best way to stress the teaching part of the program. It makes
earning or not earning a privilege less of a reward or punishment and
more of a reminder about appropriate behavior. The practice, combined with unemotional, uncritical enforcement, becomes a real teaching experience and less of a punishment. So, however boring it may
seem, make the trip to the refrigerator every time.

Sample Daily Report Cards

On pages 91 and 92 are two daily report cards. You may use these
as they are, or you may change them. Of course, you may make your
own, with behaviors that are more in line with your and your child's
needs. The first card is designed for elementary school children, who
usually have only one teacher. The second is for those who have two
or more teachers. You should photocopy on colored paper the card you
want to use. Pink is a good choice because it stands out from other papers and is easy to keep track of. Usually, the color of the card becomes a
"shorthand" name for the daily report card, such as "your pink card."
Because the child will use a new card every day, it is important to have
plenty of copies on hand, perhaps 50 cards to start the program. Since
students usually "do business" in school on traditional 8½"x 11" paper,
it is easier to use and not lose that size. You may want to copy on both
sides of the paper to save money.

**A parent must check the daily
report card before allowing privileges.**

Daily Report Card 1

Name: _____

Date: _____

Teacher: _____

Did the student . . .

	Yes	No
Come on time?		
Bring supplies?		
Stay in seat?		
Speak courteously?		
Not talk inappropriately?		
Follow directions?		
Raise hand to get attention?		
Not physically disturb others?		
Not chew gum?		
Clean up?		
Pay attention?		
Complete and hand in assignment on time?		
Grade on test or assignment		
Teacher's initials		

Homework: _____

Daily Report Card 2

Date: _____

Student's name: _____

Period

Did the youth:	1		2		3		4		5		6		7	
	Y	N	Y	N	Y	N	Y	N	Y	N	Y	N	Y	N
Arrive on time for class?														
Pay attention?														
Stay in seat unless otherwise permitted?														
Remain quiet unless otherwise permitted?														
Behave acceptably toward peers?														
Behave acceptably toward teachers/adults?														
Follow instructions and attempt classwork during class?														
Is all work up-to-date?														
If a grade was earned, what was it?														
If there is homework, please check.														
Did the youth accept the way this report was marked? (i.e.,not complain or argue, etc.)														
Teachers' initials (Please use ink)														

Special thanks to Trent Hicks for permission to reprint.

Other Issues for Ensuring School Success

As stated earlier, this chapter is meant to help parents help their children in school; it is meant especially for frustrated parents whose other efforts have failed. The program that you have learned is one that offers a good chance of helping and is fairly easy to use. Most parents simply do not go to workshops or read lengthy books. So this chapter is a compromise, and even though it will probably help you, it is not the answer to all school problems. Your child's school performance is the result of many things, of which only a few are dealt with by this program. There are other principles you can use positively to help your child and to improve the chances this program will help. There are many, but let's look at three very important ones here.

❑ *Model Learning and Academic Interest.* Modeling is the most powerful form of teaching and learning. Children follow the exemplary behavior of highly regarded adults. Or, in the words of the late psychologist Sidney Jourard, "Behavior begets its own kind." So what does this mean for you and your child's school performance? Read at home. Often. Ask questions. Show an interest in learning new things. Share new knowledge. Discuss different kinds of jobs and how you decided on yours. It is common to hear parents complain about their child's lack of motivation in school, and yet, looking at the family's own educational motivation, it is easy to see where the child's attitudes come from. If a child grows up in an environment rich with healthy educational interest, she is more likely to have it too.

❑ *Expose Your Child to Many Different Educational Opportunities.* Like the above principle, this is quite obvious. Learning does not occur only in school. Life is filled with learning experiences: music lessons, gymnastics, YMCA visits, trips to battlefields and museums, hobbies, and travel. Have you taken your child on a trip to Disneyland or Williamsburg? Both places can be educational as well as fun. Turn off the TV—don't let your child experience life passively. Fill your child's life with direct involvement. Get the idea? It is rare to see a child with major school problems whose parents practice this principle and the one on modeling. This says something about your power to shape your child's academic behavior.

❑ *Support Your Child's School.* Join the PTA. Go to parents' night. Tell the principal and teachers that you appreciate their hard work. Give them suggestions to help your child. Teachers rarely get good feedback from parents. The vast majority of teachers are very committed and want to help their students. Unfortunately, many of these caring teachers are burned out because no one cares about their efforts. Teachers get too many hassles and not enough praise and support.

Harold Stevenson, psychology professor at the University of Michigan, has reported on a cross-cultural study of schools. Why, for example, are Japanese schools more successful and lacking in many of the problems compared to American schools? Stevenson's study was large in scope, studying all parts of the school experience. The differences all pointed toward one thing: parental involvement. Japanese parents support their schools 100% and take an active role in them—very active compared to American parents. So get involved. I know a parent who gets one day of vacation each month at work and who uses one half of that day volunteering at her child's school, helping the librarian design a display, tutoring, grading tests, and planning field trips. What if every parent made such a commitment? Chapters such as this one would not have to be written.

As I write this section, the front page of my daily newspaper is reporting on parents protesting the strip search of their sons and daughters following a robbery in a school. By the newspaper account, at least, the search was done respectfully. The superintendent of the school district is being called on to fire the teachers involved in the incident. A typical event in this country. Meanwhile, drug use, personal attacks, and truancy are common occurrences in our schools.

We don't support our schools anymore in this country. We continually expect more and more from them while at the same time we closely examine their every move, stripping them of any power to ensure that our children stay on the right track. I am not hopeful about this overall picture's changing in this country, but your own personal involvement can make a difference for your child. For your child's sake, do anything and everything you can to lend support to your child's school.

Special Education

Part B of the Individuals with Disabilities Education Act (IDEA) grants federal funding to states to ensure that children with one or more of thirteen specified disabilities receive free appropriate education. The law was established by Public Law 94-142 and was formerly called the Education of the Handicapped Act. Under the law, school districts must prepare an Individualized Education Plan (IEP) for each child eligible for services under Part B, specifying all special education and "related services" needed by the child. Unfortunately, because states must label these children as "handicapped" in order to receive special funding, the children receive labels such as "behaviorally–emotionally handicapped," "learning disabled," and others. Although such labels can be harmful to children, in many cases, the advantages of special education services can far outweigh the disadvantages of the label. Often, a child who is experiencing many school problems can be helped by special education services.

How can you receive this assistance? Parents may simply ask the school to test their child for possible special education. As soon as the school receives your request, the child is usually observed in the classroom, and information is gathered from the child's school records. If it looks as if the child has some special school problems, she is tested by the school psychologist, usually within four to six weeks. After the testing is completed, the psychologist and other educators hold a meeting with the child's parents to decide if the child can be helped by special services. If so, an IEP is drawn up at that meeting. Quite simply, it is a list of things the school will do to help the child.

This meeting is also a good time to ask the school to put your School Motivation Program into the IEP. The school, then, can make sure that it is carried out in a way that helps your child. When a child is in special education and the School Motivation Program is part of the child's plan, the school cooperates and works hard to make it successful. This special attention does help. If your child is already in special education, it's easy to add the School Motivation Program. Simply call your child's school and ask for another IEP meeting to be scheduled.

When you attend the meeting, ask for the program to become part of your child's plan.

This Isn't Working . . .

This program usually works with most children, but there are times when problems are not helped by it. Often, when the program has seemed to fail, it is because it hasn't been used the correct way. If this is the case, you may wish to talk to the school guidance counselor or some other child professional to make sure you are following through correctly with the program. Sometimes, simple changes can get the program working. For example, you may not be using an important enough privilege, or your enforcement may not be consistent and unemotional. Give the program some time to work, at least six weeks. You can expect to have to make some changes in the program— call it fine-tuning. You can also expect that your child will test the program. In fact, many children's behavior gets worse at first. This really is quite normal, because people (including children) do not like to change their behavior. We like to continue behaving in familiar ways. Children will act out against new methods to try to get you to stop and to go back to your familiar ways of handling their school behavior. Stick with the program. If you stick with it, in time the new method will become familiar and more acceptable to the child.

If you have given the program your very best try and your child continues with school problems, then it is time to consult a professional: school principal, psychologist, counselor. If a child does not respond to this method, there may be an important problem in the child's life, which is causing the child's misbehavior in school. There are many kinds of influences in a child's life that can affect school behavior. A good professional can help you look at possible negative influences and take action to improve the situation. After you have dealt with these factors, then it may be appropriate to try the rule/privilege method again. A professional can give you guidance.

Good luck!!! So start now, putting your frustration about your child's school problems into carrying out the school motivation program you have just read about. Then you will not need luck; you will make it work!

**Good behavior at
school will pay off at home.**

Chapter 5
"If I've Told You Once, I've Told You a Thousand Times": Communication That Works

One of the most popular topics that child psychologists write about for parents is how to communicate with their kids. There are probably as many approaches to communicating with children as there are books calling communication the key to raising well-adjusted youths. Many of the communication skills taught to parents in these books are very useful, but most approaches have serious limitations. First, they are time-consuming and rather difficult to learn. When they are finally learned, parents could be effective in using them; however, more often than not, parents easily fall back into old communication patterns because the skills they learned are not natural. Therefore, the second drawback is simply this: parents often fall out of the habit of using their new "unnatural" communication skills.

The method presented in this chapter is easy to learn and can become a permanent part of your communication with your children. It is a communication skill that most parents can learn and use effectively, not only a select group of highly motivated parents. Note that the approach is a single method, rather than a collection of approaches that normally makes up most parent-child communication programs.

The communication method you are about to learn is not meant for every time you talk with your children. It is specifically for situations when you are teaching your child how to behave appropriately. Sometimes the method will be used before a problem behavior occurs, that is, on a preventive teaching basis. Other times the method will be used to teach the child a correct behavior after he has already misbehaved. The key is to teach children how to behave. I will say more about this teaching philosophy in the next section.

How Kids Learn

Kids learn by trying out different behaviors and seeing how they work. One thing kids like to find out is how parents react to their behavior. Misbehavior should not be viewed as an attempt to do wrong on purpose; it should be seen as a part of trying-out behaviors. In many cases, a child has not *learned* how to behave correctly. Often parents assume that the child should know how to behave correctly—as if this is programmed in the child's genes—but since most behavior must be *learned*, most misbehavior is simply not knowing the correct behavior. Parents must clearly teach children correct behaviors—*not just tell them how to behave* but also *teach* them how to behave. Since most parents have never been taught how to teach, it is no surprise they do a haphazard job of it, just as kids who have not been taught how to behave often behave haphazardly.

So, the purpose of this chapter is to teach you a very specific communication method that you can use every day to teach your child how to behave. Just as an actor has a very structured script to follow, this communication method also has a structured script for you to follow, with six specific steps. When you wish to teach your child a correct behavior, you simply put the behavior into the script and follow steps 1 through 6. With practice, you will find it easy to do.

To summarize, this communication method assumes that most children's misbehavior is due to a lack of correct skills. Therefore, the method stresses teaching behavior skills. It is never assumed that a child should know how to behave correctly. With this method, you take a positive stance and simply teach the correct skill to the child and then help him use it. In a way, this is how adults teach one another. One evening, I ordered a bottle of wine at a nice restaurant. I was surprised when the waiter gave me the cork. I just set it on the table. Yes, this was an incorrect behavior, and I should have known better! But the waiter did not react with criticism—he simply taught me how to sniff the cork and taste the wine. We do not put down adults who do not have a social skill. We teach them. This method uses the same respectful approach with children. You will always assume that the child needs to learn the correct behavior. Let's move on to how to use this teaching method.

**Assume the child needs to
be taught how to behave.**

Be a Robot

As already said, the communication method you are learning to use with your child is a very specific step-by-step script. If it sounds somewhat impersonal, that's okay. In fact, you should carry out the method in an unemotional, robotlike way. Typically, when we talk to children about a problem, we are full of negative emotions.

Communicating negatively with your child only hurts the situation. The emotionality of the situation makes meaningful communication difficult. Therefore, when you use this method, you must be emotionally neutral, communicating in a matter-of-fact manner. This includes nonverbal communication. Often our nonverbal communication, for example, facial expressions and tone of voice, is more expressive than our real words. You will need to practice in order to remove emotionality from your discussions, but after you can consistently react like a robot, you will discover that your own emotional price tag lessens. It is hard, personally draining work to be upset and emotionally charged about your child's behavior on a regular basis. So as you learn how to interact neutrally with your child, you too will be helped by being less upset and, as a result, more level-headed.

Negativity in your communications with a child may stir up two destructive reactions. First, it may cause the child to act out more in order to draw out your negative reaction. This may sound senseless, but it is a tool he can use to punish you. And second, scolding often causes a defensive reaction. If you back someone into a corner, you give him few face-saving, alternative ways to direct his behavior. Hence, he continues to act out against you. These are two good reasons to be a robot when you use the communication method you will soon learn.

Interactions
The situations in which you use these teaching methods are called "interactions," so named because you and your child interact with one another. As you will soon see, interactions are step-by-step scripts. Interactions refers to times when you use this teaching communication method. You will not use the method in all your discussions with your child; in fact, you will use the method only when you wish to teach a skill, prevent a misbehavior, or deal with a misbehavior that has occurred. The time usually represents a fairly small number of your total discussions with your child. Interactions generally take from 1 to 3 minutes. Usually you are speaking to your child about two thirds of the time, and the child answers the other one third. Interactions must be repetitious and consistent.

Repetitiveness and Consistency

I have already described how important your unemotional reactions are with this method. Two additional important factors are repetitiveness and consistency. Repetitiveness refers to using the teaching communication method over and over again. To put it another way, you want to pound it into your child's head. Children do not learn best by reasoning with their brain cells to understand and use new knowledge; rather, they learn best from repetition. You may have to teach and practice the skill with him dozens of times. This repetition will help *condition* him in the skill and will help the skill take root.

Consistency is a key word in parenting and it is no different with this method. You must continually use the method when it is time to teach a new skill or to improve a behavior skill. You can't say, "Oh well, I'm busy now; I'll skip it this time." Consistency means 100% of the time. If you can't make that commitment, then this method is not for you. Children learn best when there are many chances to try a skill (repetition) and when these chances happen every time they misbehave. Consistency gives your child a clear picture of the behavioral limits you will accept. Unless you draw a strict line, you will be asking for more testing of the limits.

The Scripts

You will teach your child correct behavior by using this communication method in daily interactions with him. The interactions are set up so that you can learn how to use them easily and so that you can use them in a consistent, robotlike way. Once you learn the scripts of the six steps, you can apply them to any behavior skill. You will always start with Step 1 and continue on through Step 6. Never skip a step. You will find that after you have practiced all six steps together, you will remember them easily. They will soon become second nature. Later, you can shorten the steps, but I will say more about that after you have learned the method.

Are you ready for the steps? Imagine now that you want to use this teaching method. You approach your child and begin an interaction. The next sections describe the six steps you should take:

❑ Give initial praise to the child.

❑ Describe the child's inappropriate behavior.

❑ Describe the appropriate behavior.

❑ Give a rationale for the appropriate behavior.

❑ Confirm the child's understanding of the rationale.

❑ Have the child practice the appropriate behavior; give feedback.

**Be a robot when using
the teaching interaction.**

☞ Step 1: Initial Praise

As you step up to your child, make a positive comment, kind statement, or compliment. The behavior being praised should be mentioned if possible. Example: "Thanks for looking at me when we are talking." "I'm really glad you got a good school report card today." "I appreciate that you're trying." "It's terrific you've been working so hard." Mark Twain once said that one should always compliment someone before criticizing him. Since your child may think of your "teaching" as criticism, it is important that you begin your interaction with a positive statement.

☞ Step 2: Description of Inappropriate Behavior

Describe the child's inappropriate behavior that you want to deal with. Be very specific: "You walked away when I started to talk to you." "You left your tools on the kitchen table." You may want to model the inappropriate behavior in order to show it to the child. You may also describe inappropriate behavior in terms of something the child did not do: "You forgot to say good-bye when you left for school." A description of inappropriate behavior can also be in the form of reminding your child about a rule he has broken. For example: "You know we have a rule against fighting." An unclear statement of inappropriate behavior is wrong, because such statements require the child to make a special effort to understand what the parent means: "You're acting disrespectfully toward me." To avoid such general statements, you should always state at least one specific behavior you can see that is part of the inappropriate behavior: "You're shouting when you talk to me. This is disrespectful." Instead of "You have poor manners," a parent might say, "You have your elbows on the table, which is poor manners." To help point out inappropriate verbal behavior, the parent may quote the child's exact words (e.g., "Saying 'shit' is unacceptable") or simply describe inappropriate language: "There is a rule against swearing." "It is disrespectful to speak to me in a demanding tone of voice." Do not use an unclear phrase such as "language like that" because it does not tell the child what was inappropriate about his language. To summarize, the description of your child's inappropriate behavior should make it clear (1) that the child did something incorrect and (2) exactly what behavior was inappropriate.

☞   **Step 3: Description of Appropriate Behavior**

In describing appropriate behavior, you should tell the child or show him the specific behaviors he needs to learn. You must state the new behavior very specifically. For example, you might say, "When you finish your snack, you should rinse the plate and other dishes and then put them in the dishwasher." This is a good statement because it shows the appropriate behavior for the child to use. Telling the child "You shouldn't leave a mess in the kitchen" is not correct because it does not describe any positive different behavior for the child. Descriptions of appropriate behavior may be in the form of questions: "Why don't you try coming down the stairs one at a time?" "Isn't saying 'Please pass the bread' a better way to get what you want?" The appropriate behavior also may be modeled: "When you come in the door, close it like this" (as the parent shows a different way, rather than slamming the door). Some examples of poor descriptions of appropriate behavior are "You should greet me when you come home from school." "You should be kind to your brother." "You should act like a man, not a baby." Some examples of good descriptions of appropriate behavior are "You should look at your brother and tell him to stop teasing you." "You should tell me in a voice level like this why you are upset with me." Remember, you must state at least one behavior that is appropriate.

☞   **Step 4: Rationale**

A rationale is quite simply a reason for the child to use the appropriate behavior. To give a rationale, you should either tell the child why a behavior is inappropriate or tell him why it is important to learn an appropriate behavior. It is important that the rationale include a statement about the natural result of the particular behavior, in its present form or in the future. If it is an inappropriate behavior, you should state the unfavorable results that follow the behavior. If it is an appropriate behavior, you should tell what good things it will cause.

Do not simply state that a behavior is inappropriate because there is a rule against it. A rationale should point out the connection between the behavior and the natural consequences; it should get to the reasons behind the rules. Stating "When you say something good about the meal, it shows that you care about those who took the time to prepare it" makes a clear connection between the behavior and the consequence.

Do not give the child a statement of unimportant consequences for inappropriate behavior. For example, "If you don't help with the cleaning, then the house will remain dirty" is an incorrect rationale. Why should the child care if the house is dirty? Below are some examples of good rationales for why a behavior is inappropriate or appropriate.

Rationales for Inappropriate Behavior

☐ "If you shout loudly, the neighbors might hear you and it will hurt our family's reputation in the community."

☐ "If you physically attack someone, it might result in injury, even if the 'fight' was not meant to hurt."

☐ "If you swear, people will say bad things about you and it will hurt the reputation of the entire family."

☐ "When you cuss, you might offend someone, who will have a bad impression of you."

Rationales for Appropriate Behavior

☐ "Doing your homework every day will help you keep up with your work in class at school."

☐ "If you thank someone for even a small kindness, the person will be impressed."

❏ "A clean sink and kitchen area help keep germs away and prevent disease."

❏ "If you ask politely, someone will be more likely to listen to you and to give you what you need."

**The teaching interaction
will eliminate the urge to yell.**

On the next page, the sentence stems will help you practice writing some rationales. Use a sheet of paper to write your responses.

Rationales for Inappropriate Behavior

❑ "If you continue getting demerits in school, then . . ."

❑ "If you are late for curfew, then . . ."

❑ "If you complain every time you're asked to do something, then . . ."

❑ "If you don't say hello to guests, then . . ."

❑ "If you tell stories to cover up your mistakes, then . . ."

Rationales for Appropriate Behavior

❑ "It's important for you to tell me where you're going when you leave the house, because . . ."

❑ "If you eat slowly at the dinner table, then . . ."

❑ "If you are polite when a guest visits, then . . ."

❑ "It's important to be on time for school, because . . ."

❑ "If you help with cleaning up after dinner, then . . ."

☞ **Step 5: Confirmation of Understanding from the Child**

To confirm that your child understands, you should ask a question of him immediately following any instructions, descriptions of behavior, or rationales that you have given him. The question must be asked in a way that encourages the child to respond briefly, even if he just says, "Yeah." Typical questions include "Do you understand what I said?" "Do you think you can do it?" "Isn't this a better way to do it?" "Okay?" Questions can also be included in behavior descriptions, for example, "Can you tell me in a quieter voice next time?" The child does not necessarily have to respond to the question in order for it to be a confirmation of understanding.

☞   **Step 6: Practice and Feedback**
For the practice and feedback step, three things must happen:

❑   You must ask the child to try to do at least one part of the correct behavior.

❑   The child must do at least one part of the correct behavior. If he does not perform the correct behavior the first time, he must practice doing it until it is correct.

❑   You must give the child feedback about his practice behavior. Here are some types of feedback:

   • an evaluation of the behavior (correct or incorrect) following the child's practice

   • praise of the child's behavior

   • saying "OK"

Correct practice and feedback might go something like this: A parent asks the child to try the correct behavior. The parent then instructs the child to "say it in a quieter, more normal voice." The child then does what the parent has described, and the parent praises him. Here is an example of incorrect practice and feedback: The parent tells the child to practice the correct behavior. The child performs it incorrectly. The parent says, "That's okay for now, but I expect better next time."

A summary example of a teaching interaction is presented on page 112. In this example, the parent assigned the child the duty of cleaning his room before going to bed each night. The teaching interaction that follows occurred when the parent checked the room at bedtime.

You can plug any problem
behavior into the teaching interaction.

Illustration of a Teaching Interaction

Teaching Interaction	Example	Reason for Component
1. Initial praise	"Great, you remembered to give me eye contact when I came up to you to start a conversation."	Shows the child that you notice when he does something that is positive
2. Description of inappropriate behavior	"It's time for bed, but you haven't cleaned off your desk area."	Instructs the child about what he failed to do or did incorrectly
3. Description of appropriate behavior	"So why don't you gather up your books and return them to storage. Then put your papers inside the desk."	Instructs the child what is expected. Breaks the task into small steps and demonstrates correct behavior to make the instructions clear
4. Rationale	"I want you to know how to clean up your desk because it makes it easier to start on time in the morning."	Instructs the child about why it is important to use the correct behavior or not use the incorrect behavior
5. Confirmation of understanding	"Do you understand?"	Assures you that the child was listening to the instructions and understands them
6. Practice and feedback	"Now, see if you can get your work area cleaned up the way it should be at bedtime."	Practice is important because it gives you feedback about whether the child has learned the correct behavior and it provides assurance that he understands
	"That's right. And your pens? Good job!"	Provides occasion for praise and, if necessary, correction

Some teaching interactions can be shortened from the original six steps. However, before a shortened teaching interaction is used, you should use the complete approach several times so that the child (1) has been presented with the skill, (2) understands how the behavior affects him, (3) practices the skill, and (4) has been repeatedly rewarded for behaviors that are close to what is expected. Used again and again over a period of time, the teaching interaction functions to fine-tune the skill. The following interactions are streamlined versions of the complete interaction.

Example 1

Initial praise/description of correct behavior

"Johnny, it looks as if you're doing a great job sharing crayons with others."

Rationale

"If you continue sharing the way you are right now, your friends will be more likely to share with you."

Consequence

"Please give yourself an extra cookie at lunch for sharing with others. Keep it up."

Example 2

Initial praise/description of correct behavior

"During most of dinner tonight you've kept all the legs of your chair on the floor. Now you're leaning back on the rear legs."

Rationale

"We've talked about how you could get hurt if the chair slips and you fall on your back. Please put all four legs down on the floor. Thanks!"

Consequence

"Please remind yourself by losing 10 minutes of TV time for leaning back in the chair."

Final Thoughts

The most important part of this approach to communication is that you always provide social feedback for the child. You must present teaching criticism in a nonthreatening, unemotional way. The interactions must stress positive teaching and demonstrations and should give the child the opportunity to practice the correct behavior. All these factors are necessary for successful communication that helps change your child's behavior.

Also, remember that it is important to give your child positive attention and praise. If your teaching is to be effective, then you must make a point of noticing and commenting on your child's correct behavior. When you praise your child, always be sure to say why you are praising him, for example, "I like your new haircut because it shows that you care about your appearance." Give praise with lots of enthusiasm, and your child will reward you with appropriate behavior.

Chapter 6
Taming the Motor
in Your Hyperactive Child

This chapter is meant for parents who have a hyperactive child or who believe they may have a hyperactive child. Hyperactive children can be quite a challenge. By the time parents talk to a professional or buy a self-help book, such as this one, they are usually feeling hopeless as well as both emotionally and physically drained. Unfortunately, there is no magic pill to help parents with a hyperactive child. As you will learn later, a certain drug (Ritalin) may be helpful, but it is only one part of the treatment a hyperactive child needs. Can hyperactive children be helped—that is, cured? Probably not, but your hyperactive child can live a happy, successful life, and you can enjoy raising her.

If you follow the advice in this chapter and stick with it for at least four months, chances are very good that you will see much improvement in your child's behavior. Also, your own life will become easier. It's worth the effort! You *can* tame the motor in your hyperactive child.

What Is Hyperactivity?

A better name for hyperactivity is hyperactivity syndrome. A syndrome is a medical problem that affects two or more areas of the body. Hyperactivity usually involves a collection of problems, with overactivity being one of several behaviors. These are some of the most common complaints mentioned when parents talk about their hyperactive children: "overactive," "always going like a motor," "can't concentrate," "slow learner," "can't sit still," "gets frustrated easily," "aggressive," "doesn't listen," "always gets into things," "hyper," "has lots of accidents," "difficult to manage as a baby," "doesn't need much sleep."

There are a number of names that mean almost the same thing as "hyperactive child," although that is the term used most often. Other names you may have heard are hyperkinetic child, MBD (minimal brain dysfunction) child, ADD (attention deficit disorder) child. These names are used mostly by professionals, and to most others they are often more confusing than helpful. They are listed here so that if you hear professional people tossing them around, you will know it has something to do with hyperactivity.

ADD is the newest name being used by professionals in this field. Research has shown that the most important issue with this syndrome is not hyperactivity per se, but "attention." ADD children have trouble paying attention. In fact, some children even have the inability to pay attention without the hyperactive behavior. Therefore, professionals speak of ADHD (attention deficit hyperactivity disorder) and ADD without hyperactivity.

One more point: parents sometimes use the term "learning disabled" to label the hyperactive child. This is often quite correct, but there are many forms of learning problems that do not apply to the hyperactive child. However, because "hyperactive" and "learning disabled" are the expressions most frequently used by parents and school personnel, they will be used here.

What Causes Hyperactivity?

No one knows exactly what causes hyperactivity. Although theories have been suggested, none have been proved scientifically. Most professionals believe that a hyperactive child suffered some sort of abnormal physical change while in the mother's uterus or during birth.

**Very active children can
take an enormous toll on parents.**

Suggested possible causes include the use of tobacco, alcohol, or other drugs by the pregnant mother; too much stress during pregnancy; and difficulty during birth, such as blockage of the child's breathing. Usually, when physicians or professional counselors examine a child for hyperactivity, they take a very good medical history, which includes prenatal and birth problems. Events later in a child's life have also been suggested as possible causes of hyperactivity, for example, a high fever of more than 103 degrees for more than two days.

Some hyperactivity may be due to small brain changes that occur because of the problems just discussed. However, it is just as likely that many such brain changes are "normal" and are not due to some physical "damage." That is, the brain of a hyperactive child could be normal, but just a little different from most brains, due to individual differences and *not* to damage. Therefore, I prefer to refer to the problem of hyperactivity as merely "brain variance." After all, hyperactive children are usually in the average or above-average range of intelligence.

In case you are interested, I will outline briefly the most currently accepted reasons for the physical causes of hyperactivity. First, though, you need to know a couple of facts about Ritalin, which is the most common drug prescribed to help hyperactive children. Ritalin is an amphetaminelike drug; that means it is a kind of stimulant. This effect seems strange: How can a behavior stimulant help to lessen behavior activity and cause a calming effect? Answer: Nobody knows—the drug is used because it often works. Here are four explanations for this drug's success:

☞   **1st Explanation**

The hyperactive child may actually be suffering from not enough stimulation in her nervous system. Her hyperactivity may be a way of trying to stay awake and alert. Ritalin stimulates the nervous system; therefore, there is no longer a need for hyperactivity.

☞   **2nd Explanation**

The hyperactive child may be overly active because of a lack or shortage of a chemical in the part of the body's nervous system that is responsible for calming down and slowing down actions. By increasing the amount of that chemical, Ritalin helps to restore this system to normal, resulting in a decrease in the child's activity level.

☞   **3rd Explanation**

A child may be hyperactive because of too much of the same aforementioned chemical. Ritalin may increase the levels of this chemical still higher, so high, in fact, that actions of this part of the brain are "swamped" and blocked somewhat. Just as a car's engine can be stalled by either not enough or too much gasoline, the brain's functions can be changed by the lack of or too high a quantity of this chemical.

☞   **4th Explanation**

Recent research has shown that hyperactive children may have reduced sugar production in a region of their brain that is believed to be important in the control of motor activity, holding in check inappropriate response, and attention. Stimulant medication, therefore, may increase such sugar production and help hyperactive children.

There is no proof that hyperactivity is the result of a chemical imbalance in the brain.

Another Possible Cause of Hyperactivity

For every truly hyperactive child (meaning with a physical reason for the hyperactivity) there are probably ten children with the same behaviors whose problems have an emotional basis. Unfortunately, many parents are scared when a professional tells them that their child's hyperactivity is emotional. Therefore, professionals tend to merely label the child as hyperactive. At least with hyperactivity, a parent knows what it is and what could be causing it. But if the problem is purely emotional, or "psychological," it becomes more difficult to understand. Parents often wonder: Does this mean years of therapy? Am I causing the problem? Fortunately, it need not be a big issue, because the approaches to treatment are almost the same, with the only difference being the use of medication. It is true that many situations in a child's life and many issues that a family confronts can lead to hyperactive behavior, but when that is the case, a program like the one in this chapter is still the best prescription.

Learning Disability and Special Education

As stated earlier, most hyperactive children have a learning disability. If there really are some small brain changes causing the hyperactivity, it is likely that those changes also influence the child's learning abilities. However, it is also true that most hyperactive children have a near-average, average, or above-average IQ, but their school achievement may suffer in one or more areas due to "learning weaknesses." Some children have difficulty with reading or writing, others have poor short-term memory, and some get thoughts confused. Most hyperactive children also have great difficulty staying on task, that is, concentrating on an activity for more than a minute or two at a time. Such a problem with attention span can cause lots of frustration. Whereas a typical child might be able to work on a math assignment for 10 minutes, a hyperactive child would probably be "off task" within 1 or 2 minutes. It is easy to see why hyperactive children usually have behavior problems in the classroom; they can't learn in the way most children do; they get frustrated, and the frustration leads to misbehavior.

Fortunately, schools have started programs to help these children. It's called special education. Years ago, "special" children were retarded children, and no parent wanted a child to be in the "retarded" class. Special education has come a long way since then. There are four main classifications now:

❑ LD: learning disabled

❑ BEH: behaviorally–emotionally handicapped

❑ MH: mentally handicapped (includes the educable and trainable)

❑ POHI: physically or otherwise health impaired

If you believe your child is hyperactive, you should request that she be tested by a school psychologist in order to be considered for special education. Simply ask the school principal, and your child should be tested within 30 days. Then the school will hold a meeting, called an IEP meeting. "IEP" is the abbreviation for "Individual Educational Plan." You will be invited to that meeting and you should attend. It is likely that your child will qualify for special education services, such as LD or EH. Either one is correct for the hyperactive child. The school psychologist will probably recommend that your child be placed in either a resource program or a self-contained program. In a resource program, your child attends most regular classes and then goes to a special class for extra help for one to three periods a day. In a self-contained program, the child remains in the same class most of the day. Usually, children are put into a self-contained program only if their problems with behavior or learning are very great. Most often, resource programs are used.

It is important that you stay in contact with your child's school. The school can develop a special program to help your child learn—a program that stresses her learning strengths—only if the school has your ongoing help. If you have any major concerns about your child's program, you should call the school district office and talk with the director of special education. This director will have had a great deal of experience with hyperactive children and will be able to give you guidance. The director also will make sure your rights as a parent are fully explained to you so that you know what to do to help your child in school.

Remember, special education is a good thing; it can help your child. Work closely with school personnel. In many cases, they will want to set up a school motivation program for your child that will require that you give certain rewards to her when she comes home from school. Your interest could tip the balance of the scale between a child who struggles each day in school and one who succeeds in spite of her hyperactivity.

Finally, your child may complain that she doesn't want to be in the "retarded class." Unfortunately, kids in school often think of all children who attend a special class as retarded. But as already explained, in reality this is not the case. However, you can't easily change that view. Your child may face some razzing for being in a special class. Be understanding and explain (over and over if necessary) that she is not in a retarded class. If the problem continues, talk with your child's teacher about other ways to handle it.

Family Supports

A very important part of raising a hyperactive child is getting help. Although you may want to get some professional assistance, other forms of support are just as important. Consider the case of a young mother who is divorced, working full-time, and trying to raise a hyperactive child. She is making it but with a very great toll on herself. Typically, the mother has no social life, is depressed and run down, and is nursing some physical problem. It is hard enough raising any child, but a hyperactive child requires special efforts, and you cannot go it alone. If your spouse is there, that will help because you can rely on each other for support. However, at times, not even that is enough; you must go further. You must depend on other family members and other supportive people in your life.

Perhaps you can do some baby-sitting swapping with a neighbor so you can get some time alone. Join Parents Without Partners if you are a single parent. This group sponsors activities and even provides child care at some events. If your family lives nearby, get some relief occasionally by leaving the child with them. You can also get your child involved in some local activities under adult supervision to give you some time away. Look for a friend who has a child like yours. Talk about your efforts to help your children and give each other support. As suggested previously, get involved with your child's school; the people there can help. You must find lots of support for yourself, or you won't be able to do the things you must do to help your child. If you're not involved in a church, you might want to look around and find one you are comfortable with. You are likely to find some support there. If you are always frustrated, unhappy, and exhausted because of your hyperactive child, then you will be less likely to be helpful to her. You must find ways to get support for yourself, some time away, chances for getting fresh again. Then you can tackle the job of helping your hyperactive child.

Hyperactive children may find it difficult to concentrate for more than a minute or two.

A final idea on this subject. Often a parent will say, "I don't have time to do that. I'm already so tired when I come home from work that I haven't got it in me to take my child to a sitter and then go to the parent group on a weekday night." But which came first—the chicken or the egg? Perhaps if that person were going to a support group, she wouldn't feel so run down. Now, you may not feel like it; that's okay. But do it. Just do it. You are capable of getting into your car and driving to the school where the group meets once a week. If you just do it, the odds are it will make you feel better. Do you get the point? At all costs, find support for yourself, especially if you don't have the energy for it or feel it's foolish. Without such support, the program you are about to learn will not work. It's up to you.

Five-Part Treatment Program

No single approach to helping the hyperactive child is the answer. There are several approaches suggested by professionals for managing the hyperactive child, and the best one is probably a combination of all of them. Following are five approaches that, taken together, provide a good overall plan for helping the hyperactive child.

❑ Information for parent and child

❑ Medication

❑ Diet

❑ Behavior motivation methods

❑ Environmental modification methods

By the time parents seek professional help for their hyperactive child, they are usually quite frustrated, often feeling hopeless. Although there are no magic solutions, if parents are willing to work hard to learn and to consistently use the methods presented here, then their child can be helped. A halfhearted effort will not do. Parents must use the program consistently, seven days a week in the child's everyday environment. Parents cannot expect a counselor to be the only one to help the child.

Therefore, the bottom line of this program is to make a regular, sincere effort to use the approaches. Only after three or four months will you begin to see positive results and the light at the end of the tunnel. What else can be done instead of all this work? Nothing. As we have already said, no one program alone has been found to be consistently effective with hyperactive children.

☞   **Part 1: Information for Parent and Child**

You have already started the first step, which is gathering information about hyperactivity. Parents often have many wrong ideas about hyperactivity, and it is important that they obtain as much information as possible about the problem. A major purpose of this chapter as a whole is to speak to this first step and provide basic information about hyperactivity. With this information as a beginning, you are prepared to make good decisions about helping your hyperactive child, instead of being influenced by some $5.95 paperback book claiming a solution to the problem by using some fad diet. This chapter provides you with the most scientific, up-to-date information available. You should read the chapter twice—the first time to get exposed to the information, the second time to absorb the ideas and to make them part of your own thinking about your hyperactive child.

We do not stop there with information, however. Although it is important that parents know the facts about hyperactivity, the child too must have information about how she is different and what she can do about it. Though they rarely say so, hyperactive children usually feel at some level that they are different. Even if you don't feel this is so about your child, she will have some difficult problems growing up, and she must learn some special ways to handle them. Therefore, your child must be told, in language that she can understand, what is different about her and why, and what things she can do to help the situation. This information should be shared in a positive and upbeat way. Hyperactive children have many strengths they can use to make up for their weaknesses, and they must know how to use them. Richard A. Gardner, M.D., in his book *MBD: The Family Book About Minimal Brain Dysfunction*, discusses what to tell your child about hyperactivity. (Unfortunately, the term "MBD" was popular when Dr. Gardner wrote the book, but it is a minor drawback.) You should borrow the book from your library. If the library does not have it, ask to get it through an interlibrary loan, which usually takes about a week. Glance through the book first, because you may want to skip certain parts of it that you feel do not apply to your child. Then sit down and read the book with your child. Make this an enjoyable time. Perhaps make some popcorn and take plenty of time. Read the book together over several evenings. However, finishing the book is only the beginning. In the months ahead, whenever something occurs in the child's life that was discussed in the book, bring it to her attention and discuss what Dr. Gardner said about it. You must remember to do this regularly. Children need to hear things over and over again. Repetition is one of the best forms of teaching.

☞ Part 2: Medication

This part of the treatment is probably the best known to parents. At one time or another, most people have heard about Ritalin—the drug that slows kids down. Although medication is sometimes used too often with hyperactive children, when used the right way, it can be part of the overall program. However, be careful—medication should never be the only help for a hyperactive child. Too often, this is the case, and it is dangerous. As you will see, medication has a special place in the treatment program, but it should *never* be the only treatment.

✍ A Special Note

My personal preference is not to use medication to treat hyperactivity. As discussed earlier, there is no sound *scientific* evidence yet that hyperactivity or attention deficit is caused by a chemical imbalance in the brain or by brain damage that in turn is correctable by medication. This means that Ritalin and other, similar medications are probably acting as tranquilizers. Tranquilizing children may not be a good way to help them. In the United States, hundreds of thousands of hyperactive children are treated with Ritalin every year. By contrast, in Sweden, it is illegal to prescribe Ritalin for the same problem. But because many parents want to consider using Ritalin with their children and because many professional counselors and physicians support its use, I have chosen to include a discussion of the use of medication in this program. It's your choice whether or not to consider it for your child. Talk it over with a professional you trust.

First, you need to go to your family doctor to have your child examined for hyperactivity and medication. In some cases, your doctor may want you to see a specialist such as a pediatrician, developmental pediatrician, pediatric neurologist, or child psychiatrist. All of these doctors deal with hyperactive children regularly; they can help you.

There is a growing agreement among doctors that medication should usually not be used for hyperactivity until a child is 6 or 7 years of age, that is, when the child enters school. As stated earlier, the main issue in the hyperactivity syndrome is short attention span. This problem with concentration can make school a very frustrating place for your child. Scientific studies show that medication can often settle down children to a great degree and help them to concentrate on their studies in school. In this respect, medication can be helpful.

Twenty years ago, physicians prescribed Ritalin to hyperactive children, and if they improved, the diagnosis of hyperactivity was believed correct. We now know that Ritalin will help any child, hyperactive or "normal," to concentrate better in school. So, if your doctor uses this method to diagnose hyperactivity, find another doctor, because yours has not kept up with the latest medical studies.

Next, some information about Ritalin, without getting too technical: Ritalin is a stimulant drug, but for some unknown reason, the drug has a depressant (slowing down) effect on a child's nervous system. A doctor will usually start Ritalin therapy by prescribing a small dose and then checking the child's behavior at home and at school, gradually increasing the amount until a positive effect is seen with the lowest possible dose. Ritalin is usually taken at breakfast and then at lunchtime in school. You will need to call the school to make arrangements for your child to be given the medication at lunch. Perhaps more convenient is the one-dose form, Ritalin-SR, which is a time-release capsule taken in the morning.

Another commonly prescribed medication for hyperactivity that works like Ritalin is called Cylert. One advantage Cylert has over Ritalin is that it comes in a chewable pill. Some children seem to do better on Cylert than on Ritalin and vice versa. Your doctor will need to see your child over a period of weeks to adjust the dose and to be sure your child is on the best medication for her.

These stimulant drugs for hyperactivity are generally quite safe, and most children do not have any side effects that are troublesome. Check with your doctor about any side effects your child needs to be watched for. The main negative side effect with these drugs, which must be checked in all children, is stunting of growth. Research has shown that some children do not grow normally when continually on the medication for long periods of time. Therefore, it is important that you see your physician every few months to check your child's height. A preventive way of dealing with this potential problem is for your child to have regular "drug holidays," that is, times when she does not take the drug. Because these drugs work very quickly and do not require a long time to build up in the bloodstream before becoming effective, perhaps you can skip the drug on weekends, when your child is out of school. Also, most doctors take the child off this medication during the summer. However, this does not mean that your child should be given Ritalin like aspirin, on an as-needed basis. When going to school, the child should take the medication regularly, Monday through Friday. Your physician will instruct you about whether your child should take the drug on weekends, school holidays, and summer vacation.

When your child starts on hyperactivity medication, try to help your doctor by asking your child's teacher(s) to send regular behavior reports—weekly if possible—to the doctor. A sample form is shown on page 130. Teachers have mixed feelings about the use of Ritalin; regular contact with the doctor will help teachers understand your child's medical program better and make sure your child gets special help.

The foregoing information about medication was written in 1992. Keep in mind that new medications become available from time to time, and studies often change our thinking about which ones are the best. Your doctor can give you the most up-to-date information.

Again, medication is not the only approach with hyperactive children. Too often, it becomes just that because it is the easiest thing to do—taking a pill is simple. But hyperactivity is a complex problem and there is no simple solution. Medication can help, but its main purpose is to help the child concentrate on tasks in school. It should not be used just to slow the child down at home so Mom and Dad can have it easier. The approaches discussed in the next sections are aimed at that.

**Medication can help, but
used alone it is not the answer.**

Child Behavior Rating Scale
for Teachers to Report to Doctors

Child's name: _____

Date: _____   Observed by: _____

Instructions: Listed below are problem behaviors that children sometimes show. Read each item carefully and decide how much you think this child is troubled by the problems at this time: Not at all, Just a little, Pretty much, or Very much. Check (X) the appropriate column. Please answer all items.

Observation	Frequency of Behavior			
	Not at all	Just a litttle	Pretty much	Very much
1. Fidgety or overactive				
2. Easily excited				
3. Agitates other children				
4. Difficulty staying on task				
5. Can't sit still				
6. Easily upset				
7. Demands immediate gratification				
8. Cries in inappropriate situations				
9. Sudden mood swings				
10. Temperament unpredictable and volatile				

Comments:

_____

_____

_____

☞   **Part 3: Diet**
Many books at your local bookstore tell how diet or allergies are the cause of hyperactivity and how changes in your child's diet are the keys to help. Unfortunately, little scientific evidence supports these claims. Perhaps one in every ten hyperactive children might have diet or allergies as one part of the cause of hyperactivity. Even though the diet approach is not the answer to hyperactivity, it may be a good idea to make some changes in your child's diet, if for no reason other than good nutrition.

Sugar is often said to be the enemy in a hyperactive child's diet. Many parents report that if they limit their child's eating of sugar, the child's hyperactivity improves. Perhaps so. Sugar has little dietary value anyway, so you should limit it in your child's diet for reasons of good health. There are many nutritious foods your child can enjoy instead of sugary foods and snacks. The next chapter, "Healthy Life-styles for Children," will give you some reasonable guidelines on how to improve your child's diet.

What about allergies? It's only a small possibility that this is an important cause of your child's hyperactivity, but you may want to test it out. You should talk with your family doctor before starting. There are two widely used methods to remove foods (and food additives) from your child's diet. One method is called a "rotation diet." You simply remove one food at a time from your child's diet and see if it makes any difference. This takes a long time because it requires three weeks from the time a food is removed from the diet before it is entirely gone from the body. If you have patience, it works. Your doctor can tell you which foods are more likely to be a problem so you can start with those. Examples are milk, dairy products in general, and certain food additives. The second method of discovering possible allergies affecting your child's hyperactivity is to put her on a very limited diet and then to add one food at a time back into the diet. Often referred to as the "applesauce diet," it requires a doctor's supervision. To play it safe, you should put your child on a healthy diet: low fat, high carbohydrate, moderate protein, and no sugar. Children learn to like whatever they eat—often it is junk food. They can just as easily learn to enjoy fruits and vegetables. This will take some work on your part because both TV and friends encourage children to eat lots of sugary foods. But insist. Also, model good eating habits for your child.

Sugary foods should be avoided.

Caffeine is a food additive to remove from our diets, both children and adults. Only caffeine-free soft drinks! Your child also can learn to enjoy natural fruit juices (*not* fruit drinks) and water. Please be sure to get the help of your family doctor when setting up any diet plan. Nutrition is a complex topic, and your child is an individual. Your doctor knows your child's physical needs best. A doctor who does not feel knowledgeable enough on the subject will refer you to a dietitian/nutritionist at a local hospital. The cost is very reasonable to talk to one, and it is well worth it for the sake of your child.

☞ **Part 4: Behavior Motivation Methods**

Behavior motivation methods are the nuts and bolts of this program. You will need to learn three different methods to motivate correct behavior in your child. You will also need to use the techniques consistently, that is, every day, with your child. These behavior motivation methods are powerful. In combination with the other approaches in this book, they will be very important in helping your hyperactive child. These are the three techniques:

❑ A simple punishment technique called "Time Out."

❑ A teaching method that structures how you talk with your child about problem behaviors.

❑ A reward program called a "behavioral rating card."

The third technique, a reward program, will be discussed here. However, before you continue, you should first learn about the other two methods. They are described in Chapter 3 and Chapter 5. Study the techniques in these two chapters (if you haven't already). It will require some work, but the techniques will be easy to use after some practice. When you have completed these two chapters, you may move on to the third behavior motivation technique to use with your hyperactive child.

The Behavior Rating Card

The behavior rating card has several important purposes. First, it is a collection of information about specific behaviors. It also shows the progress the child is making on each behavior. It requires the child to check her behavior regularly, and because it is a fairly easy method for you to use to reward good behavior, it helps you to develop a positive attitude toward your child.

This method should start with only three or four problem behaviors so that you and your child do not find the task too difficult. Look at the Behavioral Rating Cards on pages 135 and 136. The child's name and the dates the card covers are to be placed on the top lines. In the *Target Behaviors* column, a phrase is to be filled in below each number to remind you and your child of the specific behaviors being rated. Points are to be placed by a parent in the boxes when the behaviors are done correctly. In the lower right-hand corner, there are two boxes for recording points, *Points from last week* and *Total points*. The box *Points from last week* should have the number of points from last week that were not turned in for a Big Reward. (Little Rewards do not require the student to give up any points.) *Total points* should show the total of all the current week's points plus the points from last week. This box is completed at the end of each week.

In the numbered spaces at the bottom, each behavior you plan to rate should be written so that everyone, including the child, knows what particular behaviors are expected. For example, if Bill washes his hands before a meal, he receives one point. Your child should know the requirements for each behavior, that is, how often, how long, or to what degree the behavior must be done in order to be worth a point.

The number of points needed for both Big and Little Rewards is to be filled in at the bottom of the card. The rewards and the number of points necessary to earn them should be agreed upon by you and your child before the program begins. A Little Reward generally is a small privilege. A small number of points must be earned for such a reward. The Big Reward should be something important and large. To get the Big Reward, the child would have to earn many points. Look at the Sample Behavior Rating Card, and then complete your own card.

Summary: Behavior Motivation Methods

Now you have learned the three techniques that make up the behavior motivation part of the treatment program for your hyperactive child. In essence, it consists of a punishment method (Time Out), a communication method (teaching interaction), and a reward method (behavior rating card). You must use all three approaches together. Used consistently, these methods will make a big difference.

**Sample
Behavior Rating Card**

| Name of student | Bill Smith | | | From 10/1 to 10/5 |

Target Behaviors	M	T	W	Th	F	
1. Washes hands before meals	II	II	I	II	III	
2. Asks permission to go out		I			I	
3. Plays quietly with sister	I	I		I		Points from last week
4. Takes only one toy out of toy box at any one time		I	I		I	4

		Points from last week
		4
		Total points
		22

Definitions of target behaviors

1. Wash hands with soap and dry hands with towel before each meal.

2. Ask permission before going outside the house.

3. When playing with sister, no loud noises or hurtful touching.

4. Only one toy allowed out of the toy box at any one time.

Points needed for Big Reward   50   Little Reward   5

Behavior Rating Card

Name of student _____ From _____ to _____

Target Behaviors	M	T	W	Th	F	
1.						
2.						
3.						
						Points from last week
4.						Total points

Definitions of target behaviors

1. _____

2. _____

3. _____

4. _____

Points needed for Big Reward _____ Little Reward _____

☞ Part 5: Environmental Modification Methods

The final part of the program involves making changes in your child's environment in order to influence her behavior. That might sound confusing. How does our environment influence our behavior? A brief example will explain. You have probably heard the expression "childproof your room." Parents of small toddlers are usually told to store away (for a few years) many of the things lying around the house. Young children, with their normal drive to explore and touch at this age, will be into everything. Rather than having to say "no-no-no" all the time, it is easier to put a few things away until the child is able to control herself. Quite simply, you fit the physical environment to the child. Often, this is the best approach. The first four methods in this program try to better fit the hyperactive child into her environment, but with this last method, you will do just the opposite: try to fit the environment to your child. This may be a new idea to many of you, so lots of examples are included to help you understand this method.

Let's start with a simple one. Suppose Teacher "A" in your child's school is an elderly woman with many years of teaching experience. She runs a tight ship and knows how she wants her class to be and expects her students to do as she says. Teacher "B" is a young man, only two years out of college. He is full of energy and very enthusiastic. He runs more of an open classroom where the kids have lots of free time to work in learning centers. Though he does teach the whole class at once, it is only two or three times a day, for no more than 15–20 minutes. Now, here's the question: Given a choice, whose *environment* will your hyperactive child *fit* better into, Teacher "A's" or Teacher "B's"? The answer, in most but not all cases, is Teacher "B's." Many hyperactive children fit much better into a more open classroom arrangement than they do into a traditional class. As the old saying goes, "Don't push the river, let it flow." Find ways you can *match* your child's style of behavior with the world around her.

Let's try another one. Given a choice, would you involve your hyperactive child in Girl Scouts or Sunday school? Piano lessons or karate lessons? The answers: Girl Scouts and karate lessons. These environments fit better with the behavioral style of most, but again not all, hyperactive children. Would you prefer that your hyperactive child learn golf or run track? Run track; if nothing else, she will burn off some energy.

In some cases, it is not clear-cut what the *right* environment for your child is because each hyperactive child is different, with different strengths and weaknesses. Look at your child's strengths and then steer her toward environments that stress her strengths.

If your child is doing poorly in school due to a learning disability, perhaps in both math and reading, but she enjoys art and receives a passing grade in it, then see if you can involve the child in more art activities that will make her feel better about herself. You must find experiences for your child that will give her positive feedback about herself and raise her self-esteem.

Environments are both physical places and things as well as places with certain "psychological characteristics." For example, parents create a type of psychological environment. If you match a *hyper*active child with *hypo*active (that is, underactive) parents, then you have a mismatch. Parents and teachers who are mostly inactive in their lifestyle complain much more about hyperactive children than parents who are extremely active themselves. Now you can't change parents for your child, but if you tend to be the kind of person who likes peace and quiet, calm and orderly days, then you must make time in your day when you try to fit with your child's more active style.

What are some more examples of fitting your child's style and strengths with good environments? Do you make your child clean her room each day? Maybe so, but don't make the hyperactive child put away clothes neatly and have all her toys put away in the closet. You might want to have in your child's room several large boxes with tops. Then your child need only toss her clothes in one and her toys in another, and close the tops. Voilà! The room is clean.

Concerning dinnertime, do you require your child to sit still for 20 minutes while everyone finishes? This is an impossible task for a hyperactive child. You can require your child to stay in the dining room if you wish, but let her have some toys she can play with while still being a part of the relaxing family dinner after she has finished eating.

Are you getting the idea? As much as possible, mold or fit the situation and the environment to the child. Whenever you see a problem behavior of your hyperactive child (and there will be no shortage of those), before you move to use one of the other methods in this program, first see if you can use an environmental modification approach. You will have plenty of chances to use the other methods on behavior problems; try environmental modification as a first step. On the next page, you will find a number of sample situations and appropriate environmental modifications you might use with a hyperactive child.

**Parents must make an effort
to get time away from the child.**

Problem	*Environmental Modification*
1. Has too much energy in the classroom; can't sit still.	Whenever she gets to the point where she is about to misbehave, ask her to run one lap around the school.
2. Takes things apart; ruins bike, lawnmower, etc.	Go to a junkyard and buy a bunch of things for her to "fix."
3. Is too rough with family pets.	Simple, don't have family pets. Give your present pets away to good families.
4. Is always breaking glasses or dishes.	Buy a set of plastic dishes.
5. Wears out toys.	Buy cheap toys and used ones rather than fret about broken toys.
6. Doesn't take care of clothes.	Buy lots of cheap jeans and let her wear those.

How to Begin the Program

If you are ready to start this program for your hyperactive child, you have already done a lot of work. You have read this chapter carefully and you have learned how to use three behavior motivation techniques: Time Out, teaching interactions, and behavior rating cards. Remember, an important part of making the program work is *consistency*—you must use the methods every day. And second, it is important for you to be unemotional when you use the methods. Put your emotional energy into carrying out the program consistently. Do not show negative emotions when you use these methods with your hyperactive child. Even when punishing your child using Time Out, you must remember that it is important to be matter-of-fact, unemotional, robotlike. Robots do their jobs skillfully and unemotionally.

Hyperactivity problems are upsetting. They challenge your patience, remind you of the limits of your ability to control your child, and often challenge your feelings of being a good parent. This program can stop that downward cycle of failure. Stick with it.

When Professionals Can Help
Although parents don't need to call on professionals for all child problems, raising a hyperactive child and learning the methods—as in this chapter—to help the child require a great deal of support. Therefore, when you begin this program, you should also talk to someone experienced with hyperactive children who can also give you the support you may need along the way. It would be great if every school district had a parent support group. Such groups have regular meetings that parents can attend in order to learn about what works and what doesn't work for other parents. These educational groups share with parents information about how to help children with problem behaviors. The skills can be taught easily. Difficulties in parenting and child behavior problems are normal. In fact, in such groups, parents often discover that other parents also sometimes feel furious, depressed, or frustrated, which is one of the most helpful parts in attending parent groups.

Concerning the use of a professional counselor for help, there are many people you can talk to: family doctor, minister, school social worker or guidance counselor, local mental health officer, private psychologist, or other child specialist. If you're not sure whom to turn to, ask your child's school principal for suggestions. Also, your local Department of Social Services (usually in the phone book under County Government) has a child protective services unit. Call up, and this department can direct you somewhere for help.

Chapter 7
Healthy Life-Styles for Children Growing up in Unsafe Times

This chapter presents some healthy habits you would do well to consider for your family. In our fast-paced, day-to-day lives, we often have little time to stand back and consider our style of living. This chapter is meant to make you pause and think about your life-style and its effect on your children's behavior. There are many, often quite simple, things you can do in your life that will have a great overall effect on your success and well-being. Following are a dozen basic categories you can take control of in your kids' lives:

❑ Modeling behaviors for your child
❑ Nutrition
❑ Exercise
❑ Television
❑ Support systems
❑ Family meetings
❑ Dinnertime
❑ Parent-and-child time alone
❑ Protecting vs. preparing children
❑ Feeling worthwhile
❑ Psychological reactance: when a child defies you
❑ Alcohol, drugs, sex, safety, and smoking

☞ 1. Modeling Behaviors for Your Child

The strongest form of learning for children, without exception, is seeing a behavior being modeled by a trusted adult. Behavior begets its own kind! If you want your child to learn a habit, then do it yourself. If you want your child to learn a certain value, don't merely preach it, model it every day. The old saying "Do as I say, not as I do" doesn't cut it. If you want your child to have a healthy life-style, then you will have to have a healthy life-style too. Although modeling positive habits does not guarantee that your child will behave that way, it makes it much more likely.

When you spank your child, what are you teaching your child about how to handle frustration? When you drink too much alcohol or smoke cigarettes, what are you teaching your child about things you put into your body? When you spend every evening watching movies on TV, what are you teaching your child about hobbies and pleasure reading? When you are excited about the store clerk's undercharging you $5, what are you teaching your child about honesty? Now, this program is not intended to tell you how to live your life. However, you must understand clearly the fact that the way you live your life teaches your child many habits in a way far more powerful than any of the techniques teachers use in school. Many of the healthy habits discussed in this chapter can be taught to your children through modeling. Modeling is a silent teacher—a very strong influence in your child's life. So, be aware that your child is watching you and that he will learn from your habits—your life-style.

☞ 2. Nutrition

Dr. Ross Hume Hall said, "A child's diet not only nourishes a growing body, it imprints a technical way of life, an attitude towards food, and an attitude toward the functioning of one's own body."

There is a lot of proof today that what we eat greatly affects our behavior and physical health. If you teach a child good eating habits early in life, you might prevent future diseases. Right now, what your child eats can influence his behavior. So think about starting your whole family on a better diet. Although there are disagreements about the best foods to eat or to avoid, there is enough general agreement for you to make changes now. Most nutritionists agree that the best diet is high in complex carbohydrates and low in fat, with a moderate amount of protein, using white meats such as fish and poultry. The page that follows outlines some foods to include and some foods to limit in your child's diet. Be sure to talk with your family doctor before making big changes in your child's diet. Also, read more about a good diet; you might use the brief reading list on page 147 to choose from.

Your child can learn to enjoy a piece of fruit for dessert. People learn bad eating habits; they can just as well unlearn those bad habits and learn new healthy habits. You must, however, use good eating habits yourself; you must set an example. Stock the house with good foods; if there is only good food in the house, your child will choose an apple after school instead of nothing. Make good nutrition a habit. Model for your child that what you put in your body is important.

Children can be encouraged to eat vegetables if you serve them in unfamiliar forms, such as creamed or in matchstick pieces. Serve raw vegetables at the start of a meal, when the child is hungriest. Some fruits, such as peaches and apricots, have many of the same nutrients as vegetables.

The time between ages 4 and 6 is very important to a child's nutritional development. It is during this period that eating patterns and attitudes about food form. Rewarding good habits can help your child eat wisely for a lifetime. Here are some tips:

⇨ Don't give food as a pacifier or a reward, and don't take it away as punishment.

⇨ Don't worry about a child's eating too little. If your child's growth rate is normal, he is eating enough.

⇨ Set a good example. Children copy their parents' likes and dislikes.

⇨ Limit the amount of unhealthy food you keep in the house.
Have on hand plenty of juice, fresh fruit, nuts, yogurt, and popcorn.

⇨ Don't force your child to eat a food he dislikes, but insist that he
eat three different foods at each meal.

⇨ Don't be afraid to set limits. Say no to unhealthy foods, and explain why the child should eat healthy ones.

Good Things to Eat	*Limit These Foods*
½% milk or skim milk	butter
beans	caffeine
brown rice	eggs
cheese (made with skim milk)	fast food
cornbread	fried foods
dried fruits	honey
foods with high fiber content	ice cream
fresh fruits	junk food
fresh vegetables	maple syrup
low-fat cottage cheese	most cheeses
low-fat yogurt	red meats
oatmeal	soft drinks
pasta, potatoes	sugar
peanut butter (natural)	sugary breakfast cereal
popcorn (no salt, oil, or butter)	white breads
raisins	
sunflower seeds	
tuna	
whole-grain bread and crackers	

Brief Reading List on Nutrition

- Kamen, B., & Si Kamen. (1983). *Kids are what they eat.* New York: ARCO Publishing, Inc.

- Reed, B. (1983). *Foods, teens and behavior.* Manitowoc, WI: Natural Press.

- Smith, L. (1976). *Improving your child's behavior chemistry.* Englewood Cliffs, NJ: Prentice-Hall, Inc.

- Smith, L. (1979). *Feed your kids right.* New York: McGraw-Hill Book Co.

- *Nutritioning Parents Newsletter.* Nutra, P.O. Box 13825, Atlanta, GA 30324.

☞ **3. Exercise**

Today's kids are often overweight and unfit. Though many adults are caught up in the fitness boom, American children are busy watching TV, snacking on junk food, and riding when they could easily walk.

Two studies by the U.S. Department of Health and Human Services and the Planters Division of Nabisco together with the Amateur Athletic Union found that (1) at least half of our kids don't get enough exercise to keep their heart and lungs healthy, (2) nearly two thirds of kids fail to meet minimum standards for all-around fitness, and (3) kids today in general have more body fat than those of the same age in the 1960s. The National Institutes of Health have also reported a great increase in childhood obesity. Many studies show that being unfit and overweight raises the risk that children will later develop heart problems.

Children, like adults, need to exercise daily for 30 minutes, four or five times a week. Not only is fitness important to one's future health, but it also improves emotional well-being. It is very important that you involve your child in regular exercise activities and that you model fitness activities for him. Do activities together as a family. Involve your child in regular youth sports in the community and extracurricular activities at school. Try to choose sports that he has some talent for or some interest in or both. But even if he is not very good at any sport, involvement can still be worthwhile. Athletics teach discipline, cooperation, and how to handle failure and disappointment. You should contact your local recreation department and learn about the many activities available to youth in your community. If your child learns about the importance of fitness at a young age, he will carry it with him for a lifetime. Then, as an adult, perhaps he will spend less time watching sports and more time being active in them. The ancient Romans had a saying: "A sound mind in a sound body." The two go together.

☞ **4. Television**

Perhaps you've heard this statistic: by the time a child is 17, he has spent more time watching TV than he has spent in a classroom. Frightening! In fact, one Australian study reported that the television has replaced the school as the second-greatest influence in a child's life. (Parents, thankfully, remain number one.)

Unfortunately, most of the talk about TV's harmful effects on children has focused on the content of TV, that is, the programming. However, I feel the likelihood of harm from the violence and sexual themes that kids see on television is small compared to the mere fact of spending time watching television. When kids are watching TV, they aren't doing other things that are an important part of growing up and learning how to be human: participating in hobbies, talking to others, learning to do something when bored, reading, doing homework, and helping around the house. TV is a nice baby-sitter. It keeps kids quiet and out of the way but at a high price. Too much of "childhood" is being missed.

The best solution to the TV problem is to get rid of your television set. (You might want to give it away to a not-for-profit organization so you can write it off on your income taxes.) Scientists have found that lots of good things usually begin to happen in families that give up TV. Although there are some good educational shows on television for kids, there are lots of other great things for kids to do with their time. Watching TV is a passive activity; it doesn't challenge the mind. The famous child psychologist David Elkind has explained very nicely how television shapes behavior. Elkind compares TV to a digital watch; you just look at it, and there's the time. But radio and books are like regular watches; you must use your mind and interpret what you see. For instance, when the big hand is on the one and the little hand is on the three, that means it's 5 minutes past 3 o'clock. So do you want your child to be spoon-fed all his life, or do you prefer that he challenge his mind and learn how to imagine and interpret?

Control what your child is exposed to.

I prefer you to give away your TV set, as I have already said. It would be mentally healthy for the whole family, including adults. However, I realize most families are addicted to TV and won't take my advice. Therefore, for your child's sake, *greatly* limit the number of hours your child can watch each day. Check the programs he watches, and make sure they are okay with you. I don't think a child (or adult, for that matter) should be watching more than one hour of TV per day—and that one hour should be earned. That is, require that your child complete some behavior (chores, homework, appropriate behavior at school, etc.) before he is allowed his one hour each day. Also, studies have shown that one-TV-set households cause better viewing habits and improve family communication, compared to households in which there are several TV sets, which cause more individual viewing habits. And remember to be a good model for your child. That means you must limit *your* TV viewing too!

☞ 5. Support Systems

Something that kids (and adults as well) need more than anything else—except perhaps "love"—is support systems. You might be saying to yourself, "I've never heard of them . . . or it . . . whatever it is . . . how can they be so important?" Let's start with a definition. Support systems are those activities or people in our lives that offer us support and encouragement, provide feedback that we are "OK," and make us feel understood, successful, and worthwhile. Examples of support systems are best friends, neighbors who swap baby-sitting with you, clubs, and coworkers you often eat lunch with. There can be many others, and each person's list is different. One person may experience nearby relatives as a good support system; for another person, relatives may be mostly stressful. The point of all this is that kids—like adults—need good support systems in their lives. If your child does not have them, you need to take action to establish or to improve them. Before you learn how to do that, let's look at why support systems are so important.

As the name states, "support systems" give us support in our lives. They protect us from some of the daily stresses we face. They teach us, too, how to deal with the challenges of growing up. Research has shown that there is a strong connection between a person's support systems and his psychological happiness. That means as we increase the quality of our support systems, our ability to handle life's problems increases. The opposite is true also; as our support systems go down in quality, so too does our ability to handle problems. Or look at it this way: as support systems go down, problems go up, and as support systems go up, problems go down. The graph below illustrates the point.

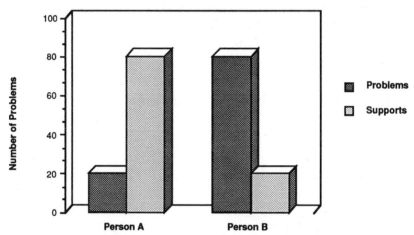

Relationship Between Personal Problems and Support Systems

The quality of one's support systems is not the only thing that affects personal happiness or distress. It *is* a major factor, however, and it's something you can do something about. The goal is not only to increase the number of support systems but also to increase their quality. One very close friend may be more supportive than five regular friends. Therefore, in evaluating support systems, think in terms of both quantity and quality. On page 153, make a list of your child's current support systems.

Each support system offers something different, so in looking to improve your child's support systems, select supports that are in line with your child's needs. For example, if he has difficulty getting along with other children, which added support system would you choose:

(1) go to movies once a week with new neighbor boy or (2) become involved in little league sports. The latter activity would probably be better for your child because it involves getting along with other children in a group activity. If your child has difficulty making friends, maybe a small weekly meeting of the local church youth group is a good step. You should not flood your child with activities and relationships; kids need time, too, to relax and just do nothing. However, two or three regular activities per week might be appropriate. Adult-supervised activities are good because kids learn about getting along with other kids and also about how to relate to adults. Some supports will require money and/or driving your child to the activity. If both parents work, this may be difficult, but there is no greater way to help your child. It is well worth the effort.

Sample List of Support Systems for 12-Year-Old Boy
✔ Mom
✔ Dad
✔ brother
✔ friend—Johnny
✔ friend—Leslie
✔ neighbor—Mr. Scruggs
✔ Grandfather
✔ scout troop
✔ teacher—Mrs. Smith
✔ piano teacher—Mrs. Harrison

In some cases, an activity may not be helpful to your child. Perhaps his scout troop has a poor scoutmaster. So watch how your child is doing in his support systems. When he tells you an activity is totally boring, check it out—he may be right.

Obviously, larger communities usually offer a greater number of activities for kids than smaller communities do. But even in small towns, if you make an effort—ask your minister or your child's school principal or the county librarian—there is plenty to be found.

Your Child's Support Systems

1.

2.

3.

4.

5.

6.

7.

8.

Another issue is: What if your child doesn't want to participate in a particular support activity even though you think it will do him good? Enough said—you're the boss—he must do it. Of course, you can be sympathetic: "Billy, I know camp can be a real pain and you'd rather stay home this summer, but . . ." Make sure the child does it.

Look over the list of support systems on the next page and think about what each of the activities has to offer your child. Then match him with the best support systems for him. If you make an effort to improve your child's support systems, it will make a difference.

Extracurricular activities are essential for children.

Various Support Systems

- YMCA
- friends
- school clubs
- job
- junior scientists club
- neighbors
- Little League (baseball, football, soccer)
- reading
- music lessons
- band
- after-school sports
- scouts
- church youth groups
- youth center activities
- summer camps
- grandparents
- cheerleading
- 4-H
- parents
- brothers/sisters
- beauty contests
- science fair
- library summer book club
- contests
- computer clubs
- gymnastics
- sleep-overs

☞ 6. Family Meetings

Any business must regularly take time out to look at how it is doing, to see what is working well and what isn't going so well, and to make changes accordingly. A family is similar to a business organization, though you probably never thought of it that way. Families can be very complex organizations, especially families that involve second marriages or families in which both parents work. So, a family, too, on a regular basis, must take stock of how it is doing. Unfortunately, because families are so busy, they often do not take the time to sort things out about how the family is doing. Because most families fail to do this, they pay the price of conflict, misunderstandings, hurt feelings, and unfairness.

Every family should have regular meetings to discuss openly any issues that are important to its members. Once a week or twice monthly is a good frequency. The meetings should always be at the same time—after dinner is usually good—in a comfortable place in the house. It should be a pleasant, unhurried time with something fun planned, like eating dessert together or making popcorn. Thirty minutes should be allowed for the meeting. Both parents and older children should be responsible for leading the meeting. It is good to have topics for discussion in the meetings written down ahead of time on a Family Meeting Agenda, which is posted where everyone can see it, perhaps on the refrigerator. When a problem comes up during the week that doesn't require an immediate solution, it can be put on the list for the family meeting. Any topic is fair game, and all members of the family may (and should) join in discussions. On the next page is a list of some possible topics for a family meeting. The meeting is democratic, but parents always have the right to make final decisions.

Although the idea of a regular family meeting may sound unnecessary to you, it is a good habit to get into. Often, families do not deal with important issues when they are left to informal, hit-or-miss discussions. Most families are too involved with day-to-day living to see their problems and needs. Regular family meetings will force your family to look at its needs and to take action. If one week there are no agenda items, then the family should spend the half hour doing something together, such as playing a game.

Set aside some time now to begin your meetings. If you think you don't have time, then that is a good clue that you need a meeting more than ever. Even if you're a single parent, with just one or two children, get in the habit of holding family meetings. It is a healthy thing to do for the entire family, especially your kids. Family business is important business and it needs to be treated as such.

Possible Family Meeting Topics
✔ bedtime
✔ chores
✔ curfew on weekends
✔ grumpiness when asked to do something
✔ kids teasing each other
✔ laundry
✔ proper school appearance/clothes
✔ stereo volume
✔ summer vacation plans
✔ transportation to the Youth Center
✔ use of telephone in evenings

☞ 7. Dinnertime
The custom of families eating their meals at home together around a table and discussing the day's events has been around for a long time. However, such family dining has become unusual in America. Many American families don't ever eat together; they eat coming and going. First, the family lunch disappeared when family members began eating at work or school. Then, the family breakfast disappeared when everyone began leaving on different schedules. Now, only a small number of families sit down to dinner together every night, and those who do are often grouped around a television set. According to a communications study done at the University of Pennsylvania, 40% of families eat dinner in front of the television.

This haphazard meal situation is mostly a new American habit. In most other countries, mealtime is still a special time. For one thing, the food budget often takes up 40% of a family's income, so you can bet eating is not taken for granted. Mealtime is a time for relaxation and family conversation, a time to discuss how the day went for everyone. Sound corny? Maybe so, but if your meals aren't like this, you are losing an important event in family life. If your family can't possibly sit down together for a meal *every* night, then save at least two or three nights a week to do so. Mealtime should never be a time for discussion of discipline or problems; it is a time for pleasant conversation. It should never be hurried. Turn off the TV, radio, and all other electronic entertainment. Talk about the little things, even the unimportant things, but talk—talk as a family. Make it a regular habit for your family, and protect it. Don't let the telephone or other activities interrupt it.

Every day after work at 5:00 P.M., I go jogging. It is a very important time for me. It gives me new energy; it keeps me fit; and it makes me feel good. Sometimes, when a coworker calls to schedule a meeting with me and my schedule is full for that day, he suggests we meet at 5:00 P.M. I say that I can't because I have an appointment. More than once, the person has later run into me jogging and has said, "I thought you said you had an appointment!" I respond, "I did; I always have a 5:00 P.M. appointment with myself!" You should be just as protective of your family's mealtime. Make dinnertime together a top priority. If you don't, it will soon die the death of busy family life. If you do, it can make a big difference. The dinner table should be a place for feeding the mind and soul, as well as the body.

☞ 8. Parent-and-Child Time Alone

Parents must make sure that they have some quality time with each child in the family. "Quality time" means a regular period of time, usually 15–30 minutes (sometimes as long as an hour), in which a parent and child do an activity together. It must be an activity that both parent and child enjoy. If one or the other does not enjoy the activity, then it becomes a time of ill will rather than pleasure. It also must be regular, at a time set aside only for the child; it should never be interrupted or canceled. Time alone is just that: time alone, without brothers or sisters. Be realistic and set an amount of time and a frequency that you can always do. Families often benefit from a calendar of each month on their refrigerator as a reminder of important events. Family meetings can be written in, and time alone can be scheduled.

Family life has changed a lot in recent years.

The greatest need for time alone is usually between a child and his father or stepfather. (This is true for both boys and girls.) With the busy pace of family life these days, too often Dad has little time with the kids. A single mother, too, can have difficulty finding time for each child individually. It is worth it, though; time alone can be one of the strongest tools to help your child get along in life. Informal time together just isn't enough for most children, and brothers or sisters are usually there.

Regular, special time alone with a parent is important.

Never use time alone for discussions concerning discipline or other problem issues. It is to be a satisfying time. If the child does not want to use time alone on a particular day, that's okay; don't force it. Remind the child that it is his special time and you will be available until the period is over in case the child changes his mind. Then read the paper, watch TV, or do something you can easily drop should he want some of his time alone with you. Even if he doesn't seem interested in having his special time, you should continue with the above procedure for several months. Often, children are somewhat cool to the idea at first, but they warm up to it later. So save the time and always have it available. When you see the results, you will be glad you did.

☞ 9. Protecting vs. Preparing Children

Do you protect your children from the crazy world out there, or do you stress preparing them for it? There is no doubt that the main attitude in today's society is one of preparing kids. We hurry them along in life, often at a terrible pace. Ours is a fast-paced and exhausting culture, and its difficulties demand that we prepare children for it. We often cope with the modern world by rushing our kids along, teaching them—often with direct experience—how to deal with it all. Consider the children from single-parent homes who frequently have adult responsibilities placed on them at a young age.

Indeed, sometimes we must prepare kids; the world has changed since you were a child. But just because our culture affects our children's lives from all directions doesn't mean we can't pick some issues we feel strongly about and protect our children from exposure to them. Protecting children from certain aspects of the world is just as important as preparing them for it. We've already discussed carefully checking your child's TV viewing. Likewise, you should do the same about movies.

In recent years, the media has helped erase the boundary between childhood and adulthood; it seems anything goes. When you were a child, if a movie studio had let a young girl play a child prostitute, there would have been a public outcry. In our "no childhood" era, not only is such a role not questioned, but the public floods the movie theaters to see children as sex objects. Our adult-oriented society has thrown sexuality at our children and teenagers. This probably will not change, but parents have every right, not to mention the responsibility, to see that their children experience childhood without being forced to deal with the adult world.

Jobs are another example of how we force the adult world on kids. Many teenagers work today (sometimes even on school nights). Researchers have discovered that youths often are harmed by such early work experiences. We tend to put too much responsibility on teenagers too soon. In single-parent households, kids often at a young age are baby-sitting for younger siblings and carrying many more responsibilities than their friends of the same age. There is something to be said for childhood as a protected time, a time when kids can just take their time to grow up. In order to form a strong, firm self-image, kids need time, sometimes just to do dumb stuff, with no responsibilities. This may sound old-fashioned, but there is some psychological truth to it. Child psychologist David Elkind, mentioned earlier, has written in his best-selling book *The Hurried Child* of this need for protected time to grow up.

So choose some issues you feel strongly about and draw the line—be an old-fashioned parent. The list might include issues such as TV, movies, violence, dating, sex, drugs, alcohol, jobs, and curfew. When I was a kid, the first parent we asked about going to a movie was my best friend's mother. We knew that if she approved, all our parents would say okay. We need more parents who care enough to be tough rather than just go along with the changing world. There certainly are times when we need to prepare our kids for a more demanding life. But remember that you should also express your values and protect your child from those things in our culture that threaten your child's childhood. Educator and writer Neil Postman once said, "There can be no childhood without secrets." Think about that. What do we keep secret from kids nowadays? What don't kids get exposed to in our society? There is truth in what Postman says; we need more secrets. Let children have childhoods. Get in the habit of watching out for your child's world. Times have changed! Take action! Protection is okay!

☞ 10. Feeling Worthwhile

What do we give kids to do these days that is worthwhile? Chores around the house or getting good grades in school doesn't count. What do we give kids to do that is really important—something that makes them feel they are needed and important? If you answered, "Not a whole lot," then you'll understand the point here.

Increasingly in America, we have continued to extend the period of adolescence. Years ago, 16-year-olds were ready to enter the work force. Many of them got married; there was a place for them in adult society. Today, we just keep putting off adulthood, and as a result we have created a no-man's-land for our teenage children—they are all grown up with no place to go. So you wonder why adolescence is such a difficult time—why there is so much concern with sex and "partying"? Well, the answer really isn't all that complex.

Conflict during adolescence does not happen throughout the world. In many cultures, kids are given an important place in the society, and adolescence passes almost unnoticed. This can happen in our culture, too.

After enjoying sports during my childhood, I took up running at age 13. I joined the high school cross-country and track teams. I wasn't all that great, but I felt important. Most of my out-of-school time was spent practicing, that is, when I wasn't doing homework. I learned a lot on the teams; I felt a part of them, and I felt responsible to train hard and to do my best. I learned good values from the coaches, and I learned to care about my health. Though my roles on those teams never changed the stock market or the political winds in Washington, to me and to those around me, it made a difference. I was important. Every child needs this kind of experience growing up. It is one of the healthiest habits you can give your child.

Remember the section on support systems earlier in this chapter? The feeling of worthwhileness is often created by those support systems, and it is very important that you involve your child in one that he can get "addicted" to on a regular basis—a positive addiction. It doesn't have to be sports; it can be clubs, school leadership positions, debating, 4-H, scouts, computers, rebuilding and racing cars—anything. Deep involvement in some healthy activity has an important protective function. Kids who have it are better off; they are less likely to get involved in undesirable things. Even when a child is involved with an activity to the point of limiting other normal youth activities, it appears to be healthy. These activities teach many things about life that one day your child will be able to generalize to the rest of the world he must tackle.

**Children need to be involved
in activities in which they succeed.**

To summarize, if your child feels he is an important part of an activity, it will serve him well as he grows up. Think about this idea in your own life. Aren't you more effective and happier when you feel needed as an important part of some activity? So it goes with youth. By getting your child on this "track," you may find that he will sail right through many potential difficulties and troubles. Try it.

☞ 11. Psychological Reactance: When a Child Defies You

So far we have been discussing healthy habits for youths. This section deals with a habit to avoid with your children. This habit is best prevented, because once your child picks it up, there isn't much you can do. The habit, called "psychological reactance," is a behavior pattern common in late childhood or adolescence. The technical term merely labels an experience that most of us have witnessed. An example will serve as an explanation: Pam is a 16-year-old Caucasian girl. She has begun seeing African-American friends, especially boys. Her parents very much disapprove and have made every effort possible to stop her behavior: punishment, grounding, taking away privileges. As a result, Pam insists more than ever on seeing African-American boys, and she goes on the sly to spite her parents.

Now, you can substitute almost any behavior into this equation. Tell the child not to do something, and in order to spite you, he goes out of his way to do exactly what you told him not to do. This is psychological reactance. When you have a full-blown case of psychological reactance on your hands, you have a problem. The more you object to your child's behavior, the more likely it is to occur. In the example just given, the family's greatest fear was that their daughter might marry an African-American man. The family's reaction increased the likelihood of that happening. Here's what's happening in the psychological reactance experience: Reactance occurs when a person sees a threat to his independence. In order to show his independence, the person resists the influence attempt and in fact may do the exact opposite. The best and most common example is an adolescent who does exactly what his parents said not to do.

So, what do you do? Back off! Put limits on the child's general behavior. For example, in the above situation, the daughter should be required to bring home any boy she plans to go out with, so her parents may meet him. The boy must be "decent" and not involved with the "bad crowd," but race should not be an issue.

If you and your child are caught in this kind of behavior pattern, in which the child is going out of his way to spite you, then you really need to talk to a professional counselor. It can get very mucky, because in this kind of behavioral situation, you cannot play by the normal rules. It will help to have someone sort it out for you and give you advice. If you try to handle it yourself, you are likely to dig yourself and your child deeper into this behavioral problem.

☞   **12. Alcohol, Drugs, Sex, Safety, and Smoking**
These are the "Big Five": alcohol, drugs, sex, safety, and smoking. They were once issues mostly for adolescents, but times have changed. Parents of grade school and middle school children now have

to deal with them. These issues cause many hassles between parents and children. This section discusses each issue only briefly. There are bookshelves full of good self-help books on each of these topics for parents.

The Big Five are best dealt with on a preventive level. Do you remember the discussion earlier in this chapter about the powerful effects of parents' modeling? Smoking, alcohol, and drugs can be prevented by parental modeling. Don't smoke or take illegal drugs, and if you drink, do so moderately and responsibly. If you smoke, you can only discourage your child from starting, while admitting your inability to quit. As long as you smoke, however, do not think that you can enforce a no-smoking rule with your child.

You should also model day-to-day concern about how you treat your body. As you model that behavior, educate your child about proper nutrition, hygiene, and the like. How can you expect him to care about his body if he has not seen from you how and why to care about it. No teenager gets involved in drugs—regardless of peer pressure—if he has been raised with a special concern about what goes into his body. Begin modeling responsible behaviors for your child, and educate him along the way.

If you think your child may be involved with drugs or alcohol, then consult your family doctor. Inexpensive tests using urine samples can now screen for drug use. Some tests can detect marijuana use up to 90 days afterward. Yes, it is worth going to that extreme, if necessary. You must be sure your child doesn't become addicted to drugs or alcohol.

Sex is a more difficult topic. How do you model good sexual behavior for your child? Well, to begin with, you can display loving, caring touching and kissing around your child. Show that there are different degrees of sexual expression, as well as many ways to be close and express caring without having sex. Protect your child, too, from the silly concern with sex in our culture. Remember from the section on protecting versus preparing your child that there is a time and a place for protection. Preparation is necessary, too, and after you have been very thorough in your educational effort and have made your values clear to your child, you must let him know that he will have to make up his own mind. Although you might oppose sex at a young age, if your values permit, you might allow access to contraception and disease protection, making sure that your child is well educated about it should he decide to have sex.

You must be very careful how you approach the issue of sex, or you may find yourself caught up in a psychological reactance situation. If you have not read that section in this chapter yet, turn back to page 163. The section on "feeling worthwhile" is important here, too. If a teenager is very involved in activities that make him feel important, then he is less likely to become overly concerned with the world of the opposite sex. A book you may wish to consult is *Raising a Child Conservatively in a Sexually Permissive World*, by Sol and Judith Gordon, published by Simon & Schuster in 1983.

Finally, before moving on to the last topic, you, as parents, must be encouraged to educate teenagers about the two new venereal diseases of the late twentieth century: herpes and AIDS. Herpes can shut out a lot of people in your life as possible partners, and AIDS (which is also a serious risk to the heterosexual population) can shut off your life. It is serious business. Pregnancy is no longer the only concern with sex. Speak honestly to your child.

Now, a final word about safety and issues such as riding in a car with someone who is driving drunk, rape prevention, kidnapping, and sexual molestation. These issues need to be dealt with directly through education. You may even want to role-play some situations with your children. So model good safety behaviors frequently and educate your child now to take care of himself.

About 22% of adult Americans were victims of child sexual abuse, according to a recent *Los Angeles Times* poll. Twenty-seven percent of the women and 16% of the men reported they had been molested as children. Friends and acquaintances made up 41% of the abusers, strangers 27%, and relatives 23%. (Nine percent was unreported.) TV ads warn of the dangers of child abuse, incest, molestation, kidnapping, child pornography, and so on. All this publicity can make the threats seem so general that parents are often unsure of how to protect their individual children. Following are some useful suggestions.

**Prepare your children; they need
education about dangers of the world.**

What to Teach Your Kids Before Sending Them out into the World

Teach your children:

☐ Their full name, address, and phone number.

☐ How to make a long-distance telephone call (both directly to you, using the area code, and by dialing "0" for the operator).

❑ Never to go into anyone's home without your permission. Children need to know whose home they are allowed to enter.

❑ If they become separated from you while shopping, not to go look for you but to go to the nearest checkout counter and ask the clerk (1) if he works there and (2) if he can help. Tell them to never go to the parking lot alone.

❑ To walk with and play with others. A child is most vulnerable when he is alone. If your child walks to school, have him walk with other children.

❑ That adults do not usually ask children for directions. If someone should stop in a car asking for directions, the child should not go near the car.

❑ If someone is following them, to go to a place where there are other people—to a neighbor's home or into a store. They should not try to hide behind bushes.

❑ Never to go near a car with someone in it, and never to get into a car without your permission. They should know in whose car they are allowed to ride. Warn your children that someone might try to lure them into a car by saying that you said to pick them up. Tell them never to obey such instructions.

❑ That a stranger is someone they and you don't know very well.

❑ Never to tell anyone over the phone that they are home alone.

❑ Never to answer the door when they are home alone. Teach your children how to call your community's emergency assistance number (usually 911). Make sure that they know a neighbor they can call if someone tries to get into the house or if there is an emergency.

❑ To tell you if any adult asks them to keep a "secret."

❑ That no one has the right to touch them or to make them feel uncomfortable. They have the right to say no.

❑ To tell you if someone offers them gifts or money or wants to take their picture.

❑ To yell "Help!" when they are in trouble, not just to scream.

As parents you should:

❑ Know your children's friends.

❑ Never leave children unattended; never leave children alone in a car.

❑ Be involved in your children's activities.

❑ Listen when your child tells you he does not want to be with someone; there may be a reason you should know about.

❑ Notice when someone shows your child a great deal of affection and find out why.

❑ Have your child's fingerprints taken and know where to locate dental records.

❑ Be sensitive to changes in your child's behavior or attitudes. Encourage open communication. Never belittle any fear or concern your child may express to you.

❑ Take a photograph of your child each year (four times a year for children under age 2).

❑ Have a set plan with your child outlining what he should do if he becomes separated from you away from home.

❑ Not buy items that have your child's name on them, such as hats, jackets, and T-shirts. An abductor could start up a friendly conversation with your child after reading his name.

❑ Make a game of reading license plate numbers and remembering their colors. This will help children recognize the numbers and letters on license plates and identify their states of origin.

❑ Be sure your children's day care center or school will not release the children to anyone but their parents or persons the parents designate. Instruct the school to call you if your child is absent.

The preceding child safety tips are provided as a courtesy by the Adam Walsh Child Resource Center of Fort Lauderdale, Florida, and are used with permission.

Chapter 8
"Today Is the Saddest Day of My Life Because My Parents Just Got Divorced"

Divorce is so common now that we tend to react as though it were normal. As a result, parents too frequently feel they can handle it without outside help. "It can be tough going, but if everyone else is making it, then I ought to too." Right? Wrong! That is not to say that you can't handle it, but divorce will have a great effect on your life and your children's lives. Many problems will be unavoidable as part of the "normal" reactions; however, you owe it to yourself to learn ways to handle the special situations that will result from the divorce.

Here's a brief example to convince you that it's best to plan ahead and to be prepared. I am the kind of person who, upon buying a new gizmo, immediately opens the box and starts to put it together, whatever "it" might be. Of course, there are usually instructions on how to put it together, but I toss them aside with the box. I usually spend the next hour fumbling through the parts, thinking my knowledge will get the job done. I begin to get angry after a while, and then when I am about finished, I usually discover one remaining part to be attached, and, of course, the entire gizmo must be taken apart to fit in the remaining piece. I have done this a dozen or more times, each time vowing that I will look at the directions carefully the next time and follow the steps. In a similar fashion, you can help yourself in the long run if you educate yourself about some of the natural things that are bound to happen in your life as a result of divorce. Divorce doesn't have to lead to frustration and anger and a family that doesn't fit together right. "Directions" can help you along the right course. This chapter highlights some of the major issues for you to deal with. There have been many self-help books for parents concerning divorce in recent years. Most are quite good and you may wish to visit your library or bookstore to look at some. Here we will try to summarize some of the issues those many books discuss.

Topics

Most of the topics in this chapter are discussed from the viewpoint of children and how to help them. However, since a parent's happiness is closely tied to the child's overall ability to handle the divorce, we will also discuss some concerns of parents. The range of topics includes parent separation, divorce, single-parent families, remarriage, and stepfamilies. Because many books are written on each of these areas and on subtopics within each area, this discussion reviews only some key issues in each, leaving you to read other, more in-depth discussions if you wish. This is an attempt to get you started in using knowledge about what is happening to you and your children in order to help everybody cope the best they can and grow from the experience.

Have You Hurt Your Kids by Getting Divorced?

How a child handles divorce is influenced by a number of things. Two major factors are the sex and age of the child. Boys, as a rule, have a harder time dealing with divorce than do girls. Children are probably hurt more in the preschool years. At this stage, a child is not mentally able to understand the reasons behind her parents' divorce.

Facts tend to get twisted, and children often blame themselves for the breakup. However, divorce in itself does not harm children as much as how the divorce and resulting changes in life-style are handled by the parents; this is what determines whether a child experiences troubles or continues to grow normally. Living in a single-parent home is not necessarily harmful to a child's overall growth. It can be risky, however, if you don't do things the right way. If you take specific steps to make sure of your child's healthy adjustment to the shock and change in her life, then she can survive and be as happy and successful as ever. Some of those necessary steps you should take are discussed in this chapter.

Fifty percent of kids will live in a one-parent family sometime during their childhood.

Should You Tell Your Children the Reason for the Divorce?

Absolutely! In all cases, children should be told the truth about divorce. When the reason involves sexual problems, parents may simply explain that "we no longer get along; we have tried." If infidelity is involved, a simple "Mom and Dad no longer love one another" will do. There is no need to bring up the details of Dad's or Mom's going with another person.

When a child is asked why her parents divorced, about 50% of the time the answer is "I don't know." However, when questioned further, often the child thinks she was responsible for the divorce or played some part in it. This is true not only among young children but also among teenagers. Therefore, it is important that you sit down and openly discuss the divorce with your children, preferably with both parents together. It is wise not to lay all the blame on one partner, even in cases when one parent appears mostly responsible. Even if one parent is 99% to blame, the other parent must have had some small role, even if it was only mistakenly marrying someone who was not able to have a committed relationship. Simply say that you are both at fault and that in no way are the children to blame.

Discussing Divorce and Stepfamilies with Your Children

The most important thing you can do for your children is to sit down together and discuss the issues that are connected to the divorce. You should never take for granted that a child knows about what's going on. You must openly discuss many things your children have already experienced and other things that they may have to deal with in the future. A good way to have these discussions is for the children and parents to read a book together. You should do this at a time when you are all relaxed. Richard A. Gardner, M.D., has written some excellent books concerning divorce:

❑ *The Boys' and Girls' Book About Divorce*

❑ *The Boys' and Girls' Book About Single-Parent Families*

❑ *The Boys' and Girls' Book About Stepfamilies*

These books are written for young children to be able to understand, but teenagers and adults will find all the information useful. Go buy the books; they are available in low-cost paperbacks at most bookstores.

Read for about 15 minutes each day, allowing a few minutes for discussion. This step to help your child with the divorce is the *most important*. It does take time and effort, but it will pay off. One final point on this "homework." Kids learn best from repetition, so you should reread the books every few months. In their heads, the children will know the issue and what to do about it, but repetition will help them begin to come to terms with it so that their understanding begins to influence their behavior.

Different Kinds of Love

One point that Dr. Gardner makes in his books is that more often than not, a child expects and wants more attention from the non-custodial parent. (Typically it is the father who lives away from the home.) Everything the father does for or with the child is an expression of love, and the child, feeling left behind by the parent, cannot get enough love. Too often, the parent cannot fully meet the child's desire for expressions of love. For whatever reason, the parent is not much involved with the child. It is this gap between what the child wants/expects and what the parent delivers that can be damaging to her, unless it is discussed with and understood by her. The child may be unhappy, depressed, angry, or bitter. She may not express these feelings to you or even show them in behavior, but you can bet those feelings will be deep inside her. Again, it is important that you sit down with your child and openly discuss this issue. Draw a long line on a piece of paper. See the example on the next page. Put an "X" where the child's wants/desires are and another one where the noncustodial parent falls on the line. Explain to your child that her father/mother does love her and that this is how the parent expresses love. Parents love their children differently, and it is important that the child both accept what the parent gives and find ways to fill in the gap between what she wants and what the parent gives. The child should be encouraged to make new friends, get involved in new activities, or spend more time with a grandparent in order to make up the difference.

In an unusual situation in which the parent fully and openly rejects the child, the custodial parent should admit this but also explain that it is not because of anything about the child or the child's behavior. Rather, the parent has the problem.

Different Kinds of Love

| X——————————————————————————————————————X |

Parent rarely sees child. No birthday cards or Christmas presents.

Put an "X" along the line where the child's noncustodial parent's expressions of love fall. Then put another "X" along the line where the child desires the parent to be in expressions of love.

Parent visits frequently. Expresses much and frequent love. Does numerous special things for child.

**Take time to read together about
what happens when parents get divorced.**

How the Single Parent's Struggles Affect the Child

After a woman gets divorced, she is often in a poor financial situation, requiring her to look for a job (or a higher paid job). While caring for the house and children, she must also create a new personal life for herself. A predictable circle of events often begins. Due to the father's absence, the children demand more of the mother's attention, but she is very involved with her new demands. As a result, the children become more demanding. Research studies have shown that children of divorce are less likely to respond to their mother's requests. The mother's frustration is then increased by the fact that the children do respond to similar requests made by their father. Furthermore, when the children do obey the mother's requests, she is less likely to notice the good behavior because of her feelings of frustration.

Are there some guidelines to help mothers be more effective with their children following a divorce? It appears that an important factor in this regard is the behavior of the father and the postdivorce relationship of the parents. The mother's social supports are also important.

For two years after a divorce, a mother's contact with other family members and friends will help her with the management of her children. Studies show that the more satisfied that mothers are with the social support they receive, the less bossy they are and the more understanding they are of their children's needs. The reason for this may be the fact that social supports systems buffer some of the stress that goes along with being a single parent. When the mother has some of the load taken off her by social supports systems, she can be more relaxed and thereby deal better with the children.

Children, too, need added supports during this time. A parent should look for activities in the community to involve the children. For example, a church youth group or a scout troop may provide children with an important chance to be with other kids under good adult supervision and to take part in activities that the single parent might not have time for.

Sometimes a single a parent tries to do everything she used to do as a family. She takes up all her time with the kids because she feels responsible for denying the child a regular family. The parent tries to be the perfect parent in a world of two-parent families. However, spending all of your time with the kids is not good for you or them. It is important to spend time away from the children.

Parents Without Partners (PWP) is a good organization to help parents deal with single parenthood. The group is a nonprofit organization helping single parents and their children. Although members must be single and must have a son or daughter, they do not need to have custody of the child. Single parents who have never been married also may join. Unfortunately, there is a common belief that people join PWP to look for partners. This is a myth, because most singles join for the many educational and supportive activities, including the programs specifically for children.

Turning briefly to noncustodial fathers, we find that they often act like social cheerleaders, planning frequent activities, such as movies, eating out, and sporting events. However, these fathers should keep things simple, doing things such as preparing a meal together or performing a fix-it chore around the house. These activities will be more helpful to the children over time and will result in a better father–child relationships.

After a divorce, parents often go easy on kids because it is a difficult time. However, it is very important to maintain firm and fair discipline. Though it may sound strange, we know that if a child is allowed too much freedom, she becomes anxious. Discipline may cause problems from time to time, but most children will be better off if you enforce rules firmly. This approach shows the child that you really care. Read Chapter 1, "Rules for Unruly Children," for more about the importance of setting behavior limits.

A Summary of Survival Tips for Single Parents

☐ Plan time for yourself away from the kids.

☐ Learn and use ways to reduce stress.

☐ Hold family meetings each week to discuss issues about the family and ways to live together.

**Involve a dating partner in the family only
when he or she becomes a consistent friend.**

Visitations should not be a time for amusement parks. Instead, do everyday activities together.

**Visitations should be regular,
predictable, and punctual.**

❏ Join a support group with other single parents.

❏ Find good child care. Check into church-run programs.

❏ Improve your own support system. Make a list of those persons you can rely on, and seek to increase their numbers.

❏ Manage your money wisely. Don't get into a credit/debt problem; it will only increase your other stresses.

❏ Make a point to do at least one thing each day for your child that tells her you love her.

❏ Take time to talk with your child each day, without any interruptions.

Guidelines for the Noncustodial Parent

❏ Visitations should be clearly set out ahead of time, in writing. This will make it easier for everyone, especially the child.

❏ During weekend visits, discipline the child as usual. Do not be "soft" because you see the child for only a short amount of time. Avoid making the weekend an entertainment time. Try to do regular family activities, with a special activity only once in a while.

❏ Do not ask your child about the activities of your former partner. If the child offers such information freely, explain that those topics are not a good idea for visitations.

❏ Never criticize your former partner in front of your child. Try to think of positive things to say, or say nothing.

❏ Be on time for visitations. If in an unusual situation you will be late, call the child and explain why. Do not plan visitations you may have to cancel.

❑ Return the child at the agreed-upon time.

❑ If the child seems uninterested in the visitation, do not show your unhappiness. It is not unusual for some children to react this way. It is really a test of how much you care. Do not reject the child for not being excited about visitations.

❑ Visitation arrangements should be made with your former partner over the telephone or by letter; generally this is true for discussions of other issues also. When you return the child after a visitation, it is not a good time for these discussions. Face-to-face discussions are all right if you both can handle them, but save them for private times when the child is not present.

❑ After each visit, the child should mark the next visit on a special calendar in her room.

❑ Avoid any attempts to win your child's favor during short visits by making special promises.

❑ Reserve an area in your house for your child's visits, that is, a personal space for her. Let her choose some special things for it.

❑ Never withhold support payments just because your former partner does not allow visitations. A judge will be more open to your arguments if your support payments are up-to-date.

Second Marriages

In the United States more than six million children now live in combined families. When parents marry new partners, hope can run high. Unfortunately, both partners usually expect too much in terms of the family's fitting together. There is no such thing as instant love. Researchers have found that it often takes children two to four years to adjust emotionally to the new family. Members of stepfamilies must also accept the fact that often a stepparent does not love a stepchild the same way as her own child. Researchers have discovered that the stresses most harmful to second marriages involve the children, the financial problems of combined families, and the emotional backlog between the ex-partners—that is, leftover feelings of anger, guilt, and so on.

The Awkward Role of the Stepparent

When a man or woman remarries someone who has children, difficulties are to be expected. The problems of stepfamily life cannot be prevented, but they can be dealt with positively. No matter what, the stepchildren will love the stepparent differently from their biological mother or father. This is normal; the stepparent must not compete with the child's natural parent. However, there are some things a stepparent can do to make the best of stepfamily life.

Ask your new partner about ways to continue family routines. Remarriage causes many changes in family life. Kids will feel most comfortable if you continue their routines and familiar family habits. Although you have needs to move beyond the past, you must remember to allow some of the "old" family life for the kids' sake.

Stepparents often experience a variety of different reactions by the stepchildren: rejection, hostility, distance, resistance. These emotions may change from day to day. You should remember that the children are struggling, and because they are children, they do not have the coping skills you may have as an adult. Understand this difference and don't take everything so personally. After all, you are the adult. Listen to the children's feelings.

As you would expect, the children will have a closer emotional relationship with your partner. They will often turn to your partner instead of you when they need something or when problems occur. This may make you feel like an outsider, but it is normal and it is not your fault. One way to deal with such a situation is to stay involved outside the family with friends and activities. Don't pout if the family is involved in an activity that doesn't include you. Instead, do something *you* enjoy. Your job can be an important support. Put new energy into it. If you find yourself becoming bitter, remember to involve yourself in important activities elsewhere in your life. Then when you do spend some time with the kids, it will be positive time.

"Name-Calling," or What to Call the Stepparent

This is a difficult but important issue. Sometimes children will call a stepparent "Mom" or "Dad," to the disappointment of the natural noncustodial parent. Older children sometimes call a stepparent by a first name, which may or may not be okay with the stepparent. In most cases, it is not a major issue for the child, but because the issue is an emotional one for some parents, you should decide from the beginning the name to be used for a stepparent. For fathers, the issue may be easy: "Father" or "Dad" can be used for the natural parent, and "Pop" can be used for the stepparent. Unfortunately, mothers have no such differences. If the stepmother is comfortable with the child's using her first name, then that may be a good solution. If the child wishes to use "Mother" for both, and the natural mother and stepmother agree, this may also work fine. Talk about the issue; get the child's feelings and those of the noncustodial parent and the stepparent, or else this issue could cause a lot of bitterness.

The Long-Distance Parent

It is a difficult job being a noncustodial parent, and if you live a long distance from your children, it is even harder. If you find yourself in this situation, there are some things you can do to keep a good relationship with your children. Below are two suggested resources you may want to get and use.

❏ *101 Ways to Be a Long Distance Super-Dad* by George Newman, is a guide that helps noncustodial parents to keep communication active with their children who live long distances away. Suggestions are offered for together-type activities such as telling toddlers weekly bedtime stories over the phone or sending garden seeds to plant as a source of future conversations. This book is not available in bookstores. For a copy, write to: Blossom Valley Press, P.O. Box 4044, Blossom Valley Station, Mountain View, CA 94040.

**After remarriage, families need to occasionally sit
down together to discuss the unique issues of stepfamilies.**

❑ *The Written Connection,* by Melanie Rahn and Jane Braun, is
another resource to facilitate long-distance relationships between
noncustodial parents and their children. It capitalizes on kids'
natural love of receiving mail. The package contains monthly
letters, large postcards, stickers, a calendar, and a creative project
four times a month for parents to mail throughout the year to
their children. The kit also includes postcards for the child to
write and draw on and to send back to you. The book offers creative ideas for using the mail to enhance your relationship with
your children. Write to: Expressions Unlimited, P.O. Box 572,
Chandler, AZ 85224.

Shared Parenting

Some early research findings are now available about joint custody arrangements and their results. It appears that joint custody families often are better at solving the typical problems of children in divorced families than are sole custody families. In such shared parenting families, fathers visit their children more often and rarely drop out of involvement with them, which happens often under sole custody arrangements. Weekend visits and summer visits are longer. Child support payment problems usually disappear under the shared parenting arrangement. Previously, it was feared that joint custody would lead to more problems because of different parenting styles; however, the early research shows that joint custody parents generally solve their problems more easily. In situations in which parents do not regularly talk with each other, the understanding that "I have my rules and she has hers" appears to work.

Anger

Researchers who study how children adjust after their parents get divorced have discovered something you should know about. Probably the best predictor of how your children will do following your divorce is the amount of animosity (i.e., anger, conflict) between the divorcing parents. The more anger and bitterness between divorcing parents, the poorer the children's adjustment; the less animosity, the better the children's adjustment. Expressed anger is the issue here. It is okay to feel anger toward each other, but just don't express it in any way visible to the children. So, if there is any one thing you can do "for your children's sake," it is to cooperate with and be civil toward your ex-partner. If you're not sure about how animosity might come out, here's a sample list:

✔ Criticizing your ex-partner in conversations with the children.

✔ Expressing anger toward your ex-partner in person or over the phone while the children can hear.

✔ Being late or inconsistent with visitations.

✔ Not cooperating to make visitations easy.

✔ Not paying child support.

✔ Not cooperating in the purchase of clothing or other items for the children.

Resources

❏ *Remarriage*, a newsletter with useful advice, G&R Publications, Inc., 648 Beacon St., Boston, MA 02215.

❏ Stepfamily Association of America, 28 Allegheny Avenue, Suite 1307, Baltimore, MD 21204.

❏ *The Kids' Divorce Kit* (coloring book, divorce quiz, calendar to track visitations, informational cassette tape with parents' side and kids' side, parent guide) for ages 3–12. *The Kids' Divorce Kit*, P.O. Box 1835, Evergreen, CO 80439.

Chapter 9
Enuresis Is Not a Fatal Disease: Helping Your Child to Control Bedwetting

Bedwetting is a common childhood problem, sometimes even reaching into a child's teenage years. Over the years, professionals have discovered many ways to help parents with their children's bedwetting problems. Parents have reached out for help because bedwetting often turns into an endless emotional hassle between the parent and the child. As this emotionally charged issue grows, a parent will sometimes resort to punishment, out of desperation. This chapter presents an effective plan that will lessen the emotional "price tags" for parents and children.

Some Approaches to Bedwetting Control

As we said, there are many programs available to parents for use with their child's enuresis, which is the medical term for bedwetting. Several of the most commonly used approaches are presented here, so that you can contrast them with the method proposed later in this chapter.

Perhaps the simplest method (and also least understood) is for the child to visit the family doctor and receive a prescription for the drug Tofranil. This drug is also an antidepressant medication, but when it is taken daily by bedwetting children, about 30% stop wetting.

Doctors do not know why it works, but it is helpful with some children. We also do not know which children are more likely to be helped by the drug. When children are slowly taken off the medication, many continue to remain dry; however, the relapse rate (those who begin wetting again after the medication is stopped) is quite high. When carefully monitored by your doctor, this treatment is quite safe. Side effects from the drug are usually minor or absent. Though the success rate is low for this method, clearly some children are helped.

Another, though more costly, approach is the "bell and pad." For this method, the parent must buy an outfit consisting of a pad (to be placed under the child's bed sheet) and an alarm, which connects to the pad and sounds loudly when urine touches the pad. Many companies produce similar alarm systems, with the Sears Wee-Alert model being one of the most economical. Unfortunately, there are several firms that market a bell-and-pad-type program with an instruction book for a very large fee. Usually, they claim great success, and many emotionally drained and desperate parents purchase the equipment for hundreds of dollars.

The bell-and-pad method involves teaching the child to get out of bed as soon as the alarm sounds. The child turns off the alarm and goes to the bathroom to urinate in the toilet. Next he splashes some water in his face to wake up and returns to the bedroom. He then resets the alarm and replaces the wet sheets and nightclothes with dry ones. After the wet clothing and sheets are put in a hamper, the child goes back to bed.

As you can see, this method is not as simple as taking a pill, but it is quite easy. Its rate of success is somewhat higher than medication's. Again, there is the problem of relapse when the bell-and-pad unit is removed, but still many children are helped by the method. It is possible to use the bell-and-pad program without guidance, but consulting a professional is recommended, because a doctor or counselor can help fine-tune the method for the individual child.

A popular method often used together with the foregoing approaches involves limiting the child's drinking liquid (water, soft drinks, etc.) in the late afternoon and evening. The idea is simple: if there is very little liquid in the child's bladder at night, he will be less likely to wet the bed. The approach makes sense, but its success appears to be limited. Although a few children seem to be helped, most are not cured by the limiting of liquids alone.

There are many methods to try to stop bedwetting.

Finally, many parents have tried punishment, usually because they do not know what else to do. Spanking, yelling, and taking away privileges are ways that have been tried to change a child's bedwetting, but they usually don't work.

If the above methods were effective with most children, bedwetting would not be such a common childhood problem. Although some of the methods work for some children, there remains a need for an approach with more widespread success. The method presented in this chapter is such an approach. The technique is not "proven" in the scientific sense; that is, research has not been done. However, many years of clinical experience have shown the approach to be highly effective. The method is éasy to use and it costs almost nothing. If parents carry out the program correctly, the success rate is higher than 80%. The purpose of this chapter is to help you carry out the program correctly.

What Causes Bedwetting?

Before explaining the how-to part of this program, it seems reasonable to answer the question "What causes bedwetting?" Quite simply, emotional factors inside the child, usually in reaction to family situations, are what usually cause bedwetting. However, a small number of bedwetting children have organic (physical) problems, and this possibility should always be considered first before following the other explanation. But 90% or more of the cases are caused by emotions.

Family situations that can result in a child's emotional symptom (bedwetting, in this case) are complex, and they differ from family to family. In most cases, it is not necessary to spend a lot of time and money to find the root cause of the problem, although occasionally, family counseling is needed. Most often, it is enough just to change the child's bedwetting behavior without worrying about the exact cause. Sometimes the change in the child's behavior produces other changes in the family that deal with the original cause. For many years, counselors thought it was necessary to change a child's feelings and attitudes in order for behavior to change. However, it is now known that the opposite approach—changing behavior first, which in turn affects feelings and attitudes—has proved more effective. These new approaches, called "behavior therapies," show much promise and have lots of scientific support for their usefulness. The method presented here is a behavioral approach. Therefore, we will not spend any more time on the causes of a child's bedwetting; we will move on now to changing the problem behavior.

A Few Background Ideas

Before we outline the steps in the program, a few background points are important.

Although bedwetting is seldom due to a physical cause, you should visit your family doctor and have your child examined in order to rule out that possibility. Usually, the doctor takes a short history of the problem and does a screening examination. If it turns up anything, you will probably be referred to a special doctor, a urologist, for a complete examination. However, this is seldom necessary. Your family doctor can usually rule out the likelihood of a physical cause with enough certainty that many tests are not necessary. The cost of a visit to your doctor is worth it. So do that first, before starting this program. Also, you are encouraged to share this program with your doctor. You probably have a good relationship with your doctor, whose suggestions will help you decide what is best for your child.

One last point about your doctor. Although we have said that it often is not necessary to know the cause of your child's bedwetting before using a method to stop it, one caution is reasonable. Bedwetting is a common problem in children who have been or are currently being sexually molested. This fact is not meant to scare you. In fact, most bedwetting is not related to sexual molestation, but because it is a possibility, you should have this checked out when you visit your physician.

This program should be used only with children who have secondary enuresis. That means that your child has had, at one time, control over his bladder. (Primary enuresis is when a child never has been dry.) Also, because children's muscles that are used to control their bladder mature at different rates, it is not "abnormal" for children to wet their bed up to about age 6. Therefore, this program is recommended only for children 6 years or older.

By the way, a useful question you can ask yourself to help determine if your child's bedwetting is emotional and not physical is this: "Does he remain dry when visiting at Grandma and Grandpa's house?" If he has spells of dryness when visiting relatives or friends, this almost certainly indicates that he is able to control himself, which brings us to the next issue: Can the child control his bedwetting if he wants to?

**Bedwetting should be a
concern to parents only after age 6.**

How Is This Approach Different?

Parents often claim that their child sleeps so deeply that he does not know he is wetting the bed. This does seem reasonable, but it is simply not true. Sleep researchers have studied enuretic children, and the results show that these children wet the bed during the lightest stages of sleep. This is a very important point, because parents must believe that the child can control the wetting. Otherwise, this program will not work.

All the approaches described earlier involve controlling the child through some outside factor: a pill, an alarm, and limited liquids. The subtitle of this chapter, "Helping Your Child to Control Bedwetting," is phrased that way for a purpose. This program is different because it stresses the *child's controlling himself* rather than something else's controlling the child. In fact, many efforts to cure bedwetting fail or end in relapses weeks or months later, because the child has not been given the responsibility for control. This self-control part is missing in most programs, and it is very important in this one. You will see how it works as we now describe the three steps of the program.

☞ Step 1: Pick Two Rewards for Your Child

As your child has success with the program and remains dry through the night, it will be important for you to reward him, in just a small way, for those successes. Whenever he goes a night without bedwetting, he is to get a little reward the next day. It must be a reward that can be given each day and one that he likes and wants. You should also pick a big reward, which the child is to get for four dry nights in a row. Again, it should be something that can be given to the child on any day that he has had four dry nights in a row.

In picking the rewards, be sure to talk with your child about what he likes. As his parent, you probably have a good idea about what your child likes, but sometimes he will tell you about rewards you may not have thought about. Listed on the next page are several sample rewards. Be sure that any reward you choose can be given just as soon (or at least on the same day) as the child earns it. Therefore, do not choose a reward that can be given only on weekends, such as "going fishing with Dad." Also, do not choose very large rewards. They should be quite small, with the big reward being somewhat more desirable. When you give the child the reward, praise the child for staying dry, and tell him that he has *earned the reward for his good control.*

Since staying dry is a sign of growing up, you should try to pick rewards that are "big-boy (or big-girl) grown-up things." The first example on the next page is a good one. Then, when you give the privilege, you can say "Grown-up girls stay dry, and they also get to do their nails. Good job!"

Finally, when you have decided on the rewards, write them on the progress chart as shown on page 198. The chart should be posted in the child's room and he is responsible for writing down each day whether the bed was dry or not. He should complete the chart first thing in the morning. A plus (+) can be used for a dry night, and a minus (–) for a wet night. You may wish to buy different colored stars or use some other sign. You should use some sort of sign for both wet and dry nights, in order to know the times the child forgets to fill out the chart.

Sample Rewards

	Small	*Big*
1. 12-year-old girl	do nails with polish	makeup lesson
2. 8-year-old boy	go swimming	activity with Dad
3. 7-year-old girl	stay up ½ hour later	help make dinner
4. 13-year-old boy	get two desserts	comic book
5. 10-year-old boy	wear jeans to school	child driven to school

☞ Step 2: Natural Consequences

The second step requires very passive involvement on your part. "Passive involvement" may seem like a confusing way to put it. After all, if you are involved, doesn't that mean you are being active? Not necessarily. In the past, you probably did something when your child wet the bed, such as scolding him or somehow showing him that you were upset. In this program, you must stop doing that. Instead, do nothing. At all costs, it is important that there be no punishment of the child if he wets the bed. This kind of reaction is often quite difficult, because doing something is often easier than doing nothing. This is why it is called "passive involvement"; it requires a lot of effort on your part to do nothing when your child wets the bed. Of course, if he does not wet the bed, go ahead with the reward procedure.

Actually, something will happen when your child wets the bed, but instead of a reaction from you, it will be the "natural consequences" that take over. So, what are the natural consequences of wetting your bed? Quite simply: removing the sheets from the bed, wiping off the plastic sheet cover, putting the sheets and pajamas into the laundry hamper, closing the lid, and putting new sheets on the bed. It is very simple, and even a 6-year-old can be taught how to do it. Then, every time the child wets, he follows these steps on his own. You should not have to remind him. Tell him that he will not be punished when wetting happens, *ever*, but that he must simply clean up. Give him several sets of sheets, and place a laundry hamper nearby.

Children should be taught to clean up the bed and to change into clean clothes after wetting the bed.

To summarize, when your child wets the bed, do nothing. Just let the natural consequences take over, which you have taught him

ahead of time. Do not scold him in any way, and tell him in advance
that he will not be punished.

Progress Chart

Reward Box		
Little Reward		Big Reward

M	T	W	Th	F	S	Su

☞   **Step 3: Statement of Confidence and Expectations**
The final step is very clear-cut. Every night, at the child's bed-time, after completing the normal bedtime routine, finish by sitting next to him on the bed and saying sincerely: "I know you can stay dry tonight and I expect you to do it." Do not say it in a threatening way; say it in a positive, upbeat tone of voice. Do this every night.

With all children, especially those 12 years old and younger, bed-time should follow a regular routine. Disciplinary matters should never be discussed; rather, bedtime should be pleasant—a time to say good night with caring and love. Within this routine, simply make the statement above, exactly as it is written, and then tuck the child into bed and turn off the light. If you do not have a bedtime routine in your household, you should start one now. That's it! Now you have the three steps necessary to start the program. Just a word of warning: if you use this program in a halfhearted way, it will probably fail. You must have confidence that you will make this method work; then it is more likely to result in success. The more we believe in something, the more likely we are to carry out the tasks necessary to make it succeed. This program rarely fails, but sometimes parents fail to carry it out cor-rectly. If you are not sure about it, you might want to get the help of a professional counselor. If you remain uncertain, then use another pro-gram; perhaps this one is not for you. If you are convinced that this program can work, then you are ready to begin.

How to Begin the Program
Once you feel confident that this program will work, you are ready to tell your child about it. Explain to him that you want to try to help him control his bedwetting and that you are going to use a new approach. Tell him that there will be no punishments for bedwetting. Review the natural consequences with him. In fact, it is best to run through the steps, with the child practicing each one as you explain it. You must also tell him about the small and large rewards for dry beds and how to complete the daily chart in his room. You do not need to tell him about your bedtime statement ("I know you can stay dry tonight and I expect you to do it") because he will learn soon enough

about this daily routine. After you have explained it, have your child explain it back to you to make sure he understands.

Every night, you must reassure your child that you have confidence in her.

Two major points about how to use this program can improve its chances for success. First, you must be 100% consistent in carrying out the three steps of the program. If you have a hectic life-style (or a poor memory), then post a note in a place where you will notice it each morning and be reminded of each step of the program. Consistency, 100% consistency, is a key word of this program. Plan ahead for any times you will not be home to carry out the program and for times when your child stays away from home (e.g., with grandparents or at camp). In those cases, get someone to carry out the steps for you. Of course, it is easier to start the program when you know these changes will not be occurring.

The second major factor is to carry out the program unemotionally. Do not show that you are upset when your child wets the bed. This will be difficult but it is very important. You are to allow the natural consequences to take over when your child wets the bed, and when he is dry, praise him. Your praise should be positive but matter-of-fact. Do not give gushing praise, just a simple statement saying that his good control has earned a reward. Of course, your nightly bedtime statement, "I know you can stay dry and I expect you to do it," should be said with sincerity and in a positive, upbeat way.

So, you are asked not to react in one case—when the child wets the bed—and to react positively, but not overly so, in the other two cases—when the child is dry and during the bedtime-routine statement. Just one last thing: stop worrying and thinking about your child's bedwetting. It may have played on your emotions a great deal, but now is the time to put concerns aside and to just carry out the three steps. Be a robot. Carry out the program exactly as it has been outlined, each and every time.

How Soon Does the Program Work?

The program usually "works" within two months and sometimes as fast as one week. The average is probably two to four weeks. Stick with it. Do not stop the program after the child has been dry for a couple of weeks. You will want to slowly take the child off the program. First, phase out the small reward, then the big one. The natural consequences should always remain, and your nightly ritual stating your expectations can be phased out after the child has been dry for six weeks in a row. If, after you stop the program, your child relapses, begin the program again with your expectation statement and natural consequences. Begin the rewards again only after two weeks of wetting.

**Your child will learn to control his wetting
rather than relying on a method to control him.**

By the way, official success of the program means two weeks of a dry bed with only one "mistake." If you have not reached that level after three months, you should talk to a professional counselor who works with children and families. As we said earlier, sometimes the cause of bedwetting can be serious, and if the bedwetting has stood up against your very best efforts to stop it, a professional could be helpful. Sometimes all that is needed is some fine-tuning of this method; at other times, family counseling will be necessary to stop the problem.

Glossary

A Note About the Glossary

The following terms are defined according to their use in this text.

Attention deficit hyperactivity disorder (ADHD): Hyperactivity.

Basic privilege: A privilege that a child should get free (food, shelter, clothing, love, and growth opportunities).

BEH: Behaviorally–emotionally handicapped.

Behavior rating card: A card used to record points that a child earns for good behavior.

Behavioral by-product: An undesirable behavior that may result from a child's trying to avoid punishment, for example, lying.

Bell and pad: A method used to help a child to control bedwetting. A special pad is placed on the bed mattress, and when urine touches it, an alarm sounds.

Brain variance: Strengths and weaknesses in how a person's brain functions.

Communication: The exchange of information between two or more people.

Conditioning: Learning that results from the frequent repetition of an experience.

Confirmation of understanding: Step 5 in a teaching interaction. The parent asks the child if he or she understands what the parent said.

Consistency: Following through with an action every time you are supposed to.

Daily report card: A feedback system similar to a regular school report card, but the child's teacher completes it daily; it emphasizes behavior in school but may also report on achievement.

Deportment: Behavior. On school report cards, many years ago, it used to refer to the child's behavior in school.

Description of appropriate behavior: Step 3 in a teaching interaction; describes exactly the way the child should behave.

Description of inappropriate behavior: Step 2 in a teaching interaction; describes exactly what the child did incorrectly.

Different kinds of love: A way to help a child understand the amount of love a noncustodial parent has for him or her. No parent is 100% perfect or 100% awful. The continuum helps a child to deal with the amount of love a parent is able to give and, as a result, not to get hurt by wishing for more love.

Drug holiday: A period of time when a child does not take medication, usually to avoid the possibility of undesirable side effects from the drug.

EH: Emotionally handicapped.

Emotional price tag: The emotional burden a parent experiences when having to punish a child frequently.

Enuresis: Bedwetting.

Environmental modification: Changing a child's surroundings to help the child behave better.

Family contract: A list of rules a child must follow, including the privileges to be earned by following the rules.

Family meetings: Regular meetings in which family members discuss the business of living together.

Grounding: Typically, making a child stay in the house for a period of time because of a rule violation.

Growth privileges: Activities that are important to a child's growth. They should not be withdrawn from the child, not even as punishment for misbehavior.

Hyperactivity: Overactive behavior and short attention span.

Individualized Education Plan (IEP): A specific school plan that outlines the ways to help a child who qualifies for special education.

Initial praise: The first step in a teaching interaction, in which a positive comment is made to the child.

IQ: Intelligence quotient; a measure of intelligence.

Learning: Gaining a skill by experience.

Learning disability: Difficulty in learning due to a problem with the way the brain processes information.

Loophole: A way a child finds to get around a rule.

Marking Time Out: A way of enforcing Time Out when away from home. A hash mark is made on the wrist each time the child violates a Time Out rule. The child serves the Time Out upon returning home.

Minimal brain dysfunction (MBD): An old term for "hyperactivity."

Modeling: Exhibiting a behavior that you want someone to imitate.

Motivation: Anything that moves a child to take positive action.

Natural consequence: A logical result of a behavior. For example, the natural consequence of a good grade at school might be praise from the parent. If the child breaks a window after being told to play elsewhere, the natural consequence would be for the child to clean up the mess and to pay for part of the new window from the allowance.

Noncustodial parent: When parents divorce, the parent the child does not live with regularly.

Nonverbal: Messages sent to a child without talking, such as by giving a hand signal.

Optional privilege: Something that is earned.

Parent-and-child time alone: Refers to a parent's spending regular, private time alone with a child, even if only for a very short period.

Parents Without Partners (PWP): A self-help group for single parents.

Practice and feedback: Step 6 in a teaching interaction. The child is asked to practice the correct behavior, and the parent comments on how the child does, making corrections if necessary.

Praise: An expression of approval for something a child does.

Preparing children: Explaining to children ahead of time some of the possible traumatic events they could face in life.

Problem behaviors: Undesirable behaviors that a child does too often (e.g., fighting) or desirable behaviors a child needs to do more often (e.g., cleaning her room).

Protecting children: Preventing children's exposure to some possibly harmful things in our culture.

Psychological reactance: A very dangerous behavior pattern in which a child goes out of her way to do exactly what a parent tells her not to do in order to spite the parent.

Punishment: A penalty given immediately following a behavior, intended to decrease the behavior.

Rationale: Step 4 in a teaching interaction. The parent describes why the child should behave correctly or should not behave incorrectly.

Repetitiveness: Done over and over again.

Resource room: A special education class or tutoring situation in school, where a child spends at least an hour a day.

Reward: Something that is highly desired.

Ritalin: A medication that often helps hyperactive children to slow down and pay better attention.

Robot: Refers to being robotlike, that is, unemotional, when enforcing rules.

Rule: A statement that defines an expected behavior.

School motivation program: Using a rule/privilege program and a daily report card to improve a child's behavior and achievement in school.

Script: The 6 steps used in a teaching interaction.

Self-contained classroom: A special education classroom in which children with similar handicaps spend most of the day getting special help.

Social skill: Proper behavior.

Social teaching: Telling or showing a child the fundamentals or skills of proper behavior.

Special education: Educational programs for children with physical, mental, behavioral/emotional, or learning handicaps.

Support systems: Activities and people in our lives that offer support and encouragement; they offer feedback that we are "OK," and they make us feel understood, successful, and worthwhile.

Target behaviors: The specific behaviors you choose to change by using a discipline program.

Teaching interaction: A step-by-step way of teaching a child a social skill.

Testing behavior: The normal behavior of children when they break new rules to "test out" what will really happen as a consequence.

Time Out: A mild but effective form of punishment in which the child must remain in a very boring place for a short period of time. The term means "time out" from all rewarding things.

Time Out rule: A rule that, if violated, results in Time Out for the child.

Token: Something such as a certificate or a chip that a child earns for good behavior and can exchange later for a desired reward.

What ifs: Situations that commonly occur when you start to use a new discipline approach with your child.

Index

NATIONAL UNIVERSITY
LIBRARY   SAN DIEGO

6128

6128